D1433171

THE OFFICIAL ARRSE GUIDE TO THE BRITISH ARMY

www.transworldbooks.co.uk

WWW.ARRSE.CO.UK

THE OFFICIAL ARRSE GUIDE TO THE BRITISH ARMY

What it is and how it works

Compiled by

MAJOR DES ASTOR

BANTAM PRESS

LONDON · TORONTO · SYDNEY · AUCKLAND · JOHANNESBURG

TRANSWORLD PUBLISHERS
61–63 Uxbridge Road, London W5 5SA
A Random House Group Company
www.transworldbooks.co.uk

First published in Great Britain
in 2011 by Bantam Press
an imprint of Transworld Publishers

Designed by Nick Avery Design

A CIP catalogue record for this book
is available from the British Library.

ISBN 9780593065617

Addresses for Random House Group Ltd companies outside the UK
can be found at: www.randomhouse.co.uk
The Random House Group Ltd Reg. No. 954009

The Random House Group Limited supports The Forest Stewardship
Council (FSC®), the leading international forest certification
organization. Our books carrying the FSC label are printed on FSC®
certified paper. FSC is the only forest certification scheme endorsed by
the leading environmental organizations, including Greenpeace. Our
paper procurement policy can be found at www.randomhouse.co.uk/
environment.

Typeset in Plantin
Printed and bound in by MPG

2 4 6 8 10 9 7 5 3 1

CONTENTS

6 FOREWORD

8 AN INTRODUCTION TO ARRSE

10 WHAT THE BRITISH ARMY IS, AND HOW IT WORKS

12 COMBAT ARMS

28 RECRUITMENT

52 TRAINING

62 THE KIT

108 WHO'S WHO

138 COMBAT SUPPORT ARMS

160 ARMY PLACES

168 COMBAT SERVICE SUPPORT

186 FORMATIONS

192 THE WEIRD AND WONDERFUL WORLD OF WALTS

200 THE OTHER SERVICES

214 APPENDIX: MULTI-LETTER ACRONYMS

220 ABOUT THE AUTHOR

222 ACKNOWLEDGEMENTS

FOREWORD

by Lieutenant General Sir Hector
Clench, KCB DSO MBE
C-in-C, Joint Cyberspace Command

I don't imagine it will come as any great surprise to readers of this book that the Army was initially wary of embracing the concept of 'Arrse', websites like it and, indeed, of the world wide net as a whole. I can honestly say that back in 2004, when I was first appointed to head the scoping team for future Army digitification, it took an immense amount of lobbying on my part of ministers, service chiefs, senior officials and, of course, my very good friends in the defence industry – whom one will, one hopes, be joining shortly after one's formal retirement from the service – to ensure that requirements were identified, funds released and equipment procured to make certain that 'Defence' was at the forefront of the electrical age.

I feel a certain amount of – I hope justifiable – pride that as Director General Defence Network Capability I was the first officer of two-star rank or above to have an official 'email' address and that, since that exciting day in 2007, Miss Sherrard, my PA, has been able to send and receive 'email' on my behalf at an astonishing rate (once they've been through the usual staffing, checking and red-inking procedure involving my Chief of Staff, the SO1 J6 and Staff Sergeant Hobsbawm, who knows about computers). It's a sign of the times that a memo or letter which might have taken 10 days from first draft to release in the old 'snail mail' era can now be 'good to go' in 8 days or less as an 'email', with no more than a 20% increase in our manpower bill.

But the white heat of progress comes at a cost. When we started Project DIGIT, ministers were rightly insistent that as much of the spend as possible, right across the piece, should come from commercial off-the-shelf sources. Sadly, this proved impossible. After much lobbying from industry, we realized that operating systems like Windows™, Unix and Linux were hopelessly insecure and the first part of the project involved the development – by a consortium of European defence contractors – of our own powerful, bespoke platform called 'DefenceDoorways'. Despite the 42% cost overrun, I am confident that when finished this will prove to be £12 billion well spent, especially after we have developed the tools to enable our hardware to communicate with the Windows™ based systems of our allies.

Of course, in this 'digital' age, computers aren't just about work. I'm told that it is possible to play games, read newspapers, buy books and even 'chat' if you plug them in to the 'net'. Staff Sergeant Hobsbawm has recently taught me 'Solitaire' (a computerized version of patience) on my state-of-the-art secure laptop and as soon as I get it back from lost property I shall be getting some practice in.

Entertainment is what Arrse – The Army Rumour Service, to give it its polite name – is all about. It's absolutely marvellous that the soldiers can have what they call 'a laugh', and we at the top of the military hierarchy are very keen that they should continue to do so. It's just a shame it has to be accompanied by all that griping and by what are, let's face it, some exhibitions of very questionable taste indeed. Nevertheless, once we have identified the ringleaders and taken action – including but not limited to AGAI 67 – against them, I'm sure we will be happy to endorse it, albeit in a limited way.

It is no surprise to me that Des Astor is involved in this project. I first encountered Major Astor as a subaltern in my company in Osnabruck in 1976. We were, I dare say, a pretty cosmopolitan Officers' Mess in the Loamshires back then. Chaps came from all kinds of backgrounds, ranging from the traditional – Eton and Winchester – to the frankly outré: Wellington, Charterhouse and one, you may find it hard to believe, from Stowe (although, to be fair, he didn't last long). Despite this, Des was something of a 'coloured person' in this particularly diverse woodpile, with his unusual north Midlands accent and Bri-nylon shirts. It's a tribute to his determination and, admittedly, thick skin, that he stuck with it and forged a career despite the open hostility of officers, soldiers and chain of command. In a meritocratic hierarchy like the Army, we can't all reach the top, but to give credit where it's due, Des Astor gave it his best shot. The fact that he fell well short of the required standard is by the by. Doubtless his involvement with Arrse gives him a sense of fulfilment he is unable to obtain elsewhere.

So, slightly caveated, I commend his book to you. I have yet to read it myself, but Major Astor has assured me that it is an amusing and affectionate introduction to some of the finer points of life in the British Army. If this is indeed the case, then, up to a point, he need have nothing to fear.

H P R N Clench
Lt Gen
HQ Cyber Command

November 2011

AN INTRODUCTION TO ARRSE

Like so many good things, Arrse was the product of a beer-fuelled pub conversation between friends.

It so happens that this one took place on Christmas Eve 2000. One participant, known only by the cover name 'Adjutant', expounded a theory that an internet discussion forum like the 'Professional Pilots Rumour Network' (PPRuNe) might be popular in the Army. His co-conspirators (the artists now known and feared as Good CO and Bad CO) thought about this, scratched their heads, rearranged their testicles, bought a book about HTML from PC World and, in the new year, ARRSE was born.

With a rudimentary form of Arrse online not long afterwards, many of the early members were poached from among military users of PPRuNe, which explains why, in the early days at least, there was quite a strong flavour of the Army Air Corps about the site. At this stage, the biggest boost Arrse received was the decision (since rescinded) to block Arrse from the network at the Joint Services Command and Staff College – fantastic free publicity among the target audience!

Traffic on Arrse steadily built over the next couple of years with, oddly enough, events like the invasion of Iraq helping to build membership by spreading the word outside the fairly narrow circles who had been hitherto using the site. It so happens that I was first shown it by a REME officer on a satellite internet terminal in southern Iraq in July 2003.

But the first really major boost to Arrse came about in May 2004 when the *Daily Mirror*, under editor Piers Morgan, bought and published photographs allegedly showing soldiers of the Queen's Lancashire Regiment abusing Iraqi prisoners in the back of a truck. Thanks to some sharp-eyed Arrsers – led initially by ViroBono – suspicions were soon raised and it quickly emerged that (a) the pictures

had been taken at a TA centre in north-west England, and (b) Morgan and the *Mirror* had made no serious attempt to check their veracity. Uh-oh. Amid a storm of public anger, Morgan was unceremoniously dumped from his job. Bye-bye Piers! Since the egregious Morgan bought it at the *Mirror* Arrse has led several high-profile campaigns, including: securing a change in the law which had disenfranchised thousands of British service personnel before the 2005 general election; forcing Tony Blair to back General Sir Richard Dannatt, the then Chief of the General Staff, when he spoke out about the pressure of fighting two underfunded wars; the creation of the British Armed Forces Federation, the new and surprisingly influential staff association for Armed Forces Personnel; rights of UK residence being granted to Tulbahadur Pun VC, the World War Two Gurkha veteran; the fight to allow a house for wounded soldiers' relatives to be converted next to the Rehabilitation Centre at Headley Court.

The Piers Morgan affair established Arrse in the eyes of the UK media as the go-to website for up-to-date inside information from the Army and this has been the case ever since: when a journalist wants to know how to skiff his editor, whether soldiers are really talking about the early English king Cnut when they're bantering with each other, or even what soldiers' opinions are about the latest round of defence cuts, Arrse is the first place they come to. Read on to find out why . . .

WHAT THE BRITISH ARMY IS, AND HOW IT WORKS

The first time you meet members of the British Army, you could easily be forgiven for thinking that rather than a big cohesive whole, what you've actually come across is a group of fiercely xenophobic independent tribes who all happen to buy their clothes at the same shop. It's not far from the truth. The regimental system is one of the biggest strengths of the Army but it's also a source of friction. Partly this is role snobbery: being a Tom in the Parachute Regiment is way more 'ally' than being a technician in the Royal Army Dental Corps (even though it's the Army's only real 'teeth' arm). Partly it's social: you can find some frightfully grand officers in the Household Division and some of the line cavalry regiments, rather fewer in the Mercian Regiment or the REME (though they do have a rogue Earl lurking up their sleeves – and he started out as a private soldier).

"TWO TYPES" by JON

The army: cruelly accurate stereotypes over many decades.

The easiest way to look at the regimental system is by role, and the Army does this by splitting the regiments and corps into Combat Arms (the people who do the actual fighting), Combat Support Arms (the guys who operate in direct support of the fighting soldiers) and Combat Service Support (the people who provide the logistic, materiel, maintenance and medical support).

Before we leap in, a word on regimental nicknames. The ones quoted here are generally what other units within the Army call them, not what they call themselves. If that was the case, every single unit in the Army would have the nickname 'Huge-cocked Supermen and their Glamorous Assistants', and that just wouldn't be credible, now would it? It's also worth noting that some regiments have been amalgamated so many times recently that their old nicknames have become meaningless and they have yet to attract new ones. Finally, almost any regiment that recruits from mainly rural areas, like Wales and the Highlands of Scotland, will have to live with accusations of animal molestation: it goes with the territory, so to speak.

Popular with rural regiments.

COMBAT ARMS

Loosely defined as the bits of the Army which engage the enemy with direct-fire weapons.

THE ROYAL ARMOURED CORPS

The first of these is the Royal Armoured Corps or RAC (not to be confused with the motoring organization of the same initials, or even the slightly naff London 'gentlemen's' club). There are basically four elements to the RAC: the Household Cavalry, the line cavalry, the Royal Tank Regiment and the Yeomanry – although, of course, in true British Army style, the Household Cav will tell you they aren't actually part of the RAC but a separate corps in their own right.

These regiments have three basic roles: formation reconnaissance, armoured, and CBRN recce.

1 **Formation Recce** This is pretty much the same role that light cavalry have always had. In high-intensity war-fighting, formation recce regiments push out in front of and to the flanks of the formations (brigade or division) they are supporting in order to gather information, locate the enemy, and (many claim) hold dazzling cocktail parties. They traded in their horses for armoured vehicles some time ago and their current steeds are, by and large, the CVR(T) family of light tracked vehicles, primarily the Scimitar, although they are also trained to operate on foot, which is often more appropriate, particularly in counter-insurgency campaigns like Afghanistan. As well as information gathering, formation recce has the capability to call in mortar, artillery and air support, and they can engage enemies with their own anti-armour capabilities, so it isn't just about wetting their pants and running home to Mummy when the enemy come into sight.

2 Armoured The armoured role is all about driving around in huge fuck-off Challenger 2 main battle tanks, crushing screaming infantrymen beneath your tracks (many of whom will be members of enemy forces) and blowing large fatal holes in huge fuck-off enemy main battle tanks, armoured personnel carriers and vehicles of all descriptions. Which is fun.

3 CBRN Recce 'Chemical, Biological, Radiological and Nuclear', better known to soldiers *d'un certain âge* as 'NBC', is done by a joint regiment made up from 1 RTR and some Rock Apes from the RAF Regiment. Sadly the role is basically only to detect, recce, survey and report on the opposition's chemical weapons rather than rain high-tech death upon the enemies of the Queen, but you never know your luck. The basic vehicle they do this from is the German-made Fuchs (fnarr, fnarr).

THE HOUSEHOLD CAVALRY
The Donkey Wallopers; the Tin Bellies; the Cheesemongers; the Oxford Blues; the Piccadilly Cowboys; the Bird-catchers

The Household Cavalry are a 'union' (not an amalgamation) of the Life Guards and the Blues and Royals which together form two regiments: the Household Cavalry Regiment (HCR), based at Combermere Barracks, Windsor, which is a formation recce regiment; and the Household Cavalry Mounted Regiment, based at Knightsbridge Barracks in central London, which provides ceremonial mounted cavalry (and a mounted band) for escorting the Queen, and guards HQ London District in Whitehall (aka 'Horse Guards') – basically trotting about looking smart on state occasions and generally impressing Johnny Foreigner (except, obviously, the French, who aren't going to be impressed by anything the British Army gets up to, no matter how shiny we make it).

Think polish.

Traditionally, these are the two poshest regiments in the British Army. By reputation, the Life Guards attract the richest officers while the Blues and Royals attract the socially grandest, but if this distinction was ever true it has all but evaporated these days (except, of course, as you may have noticed, a couple of princes joined the Blues and Royals rather than the Life Guards). Soldiers tend to be a mixture of those who join because they want to work with horses, those who are attracted to ceremony, and those who are interested in the armoured recce role. The HCR's role is

Jolly banter from 3 Para.

formation recce for 3 UK Division, the deployable division based at Bulford in Wiltshire, but its D Squadron is trained to work directly with 16 Air Assault Brigade, and as a result a good few officers and soldiers, though no horses, get to do P Company and the Para course.

One of the oddities about the Household Cav is their rank system. For reasons too boring to discuss, Sergeants in the Household Cavalry are called 'Corporals of Horse' and Sergeant Majors become 'Corporal Majors'. Equally strangely, Second Lieutenants are called 'Cornets', although there is no truth in the rumour that Lieutenants are known as 'Mivvies'; the assistant adjutant may or may not be a '99'. One of the most distinctive features of the Household Cavalry Mounted Regiment is that it is the last bit of the Army which still wears shiny metal armour. Looks great, eh? (Hint: someone has to polish it . . .)

THE LINE CAVALRY

A fraction less socially grand than the Household Cav but still feeling pretty pleased with themselves are the line cavalry regiments. A brutal round of amalgamations circa 1993 did for several of the remaining famous names, including most of the 'vulgar fractions', without doing a lot to alter the essential character of the regiments as refuges for minor public school officers with social ambitions.

1st The Queen's Dragoon Guards
The Welsh Cavalry (allegedly, though I've never heard them called this outside recruiting material; nicknames referring to sheep-shagging are probably more realistic); the Queen's Dancing Girls

The QDG, the senior line cavalry regiment, were formed in 1959 by amalgamating the King's Dragoon Guards and the Bays. The soldiers of the QDG are primarily recruited from Wales, Herefordshire and Shropshire, while the officers are recruited from among people who may have occasionally visited Wales, Herefordshire and Shropshire, or at least know some people who have.

The QDG are currently based in Sennelager near Paderborn, north Germany, which at least means they have access to (a) skiing, (b) duty frees, (c) LOA, and (d) Tingle-Tangles knocking shop on the Sennelager strip. Junior ranks have Gucci-modernized accommodation in Dempsey Barracks. Doubtless having spent gazillions on fixing it up, we'll hand it over to the Krauts for nothing at some point in the next few years.

The QDG role is to provide formation recce for 20 Armoured Brigade, which forms part of 1 UK Armoured Division, but their last deployment was doing recce in Afghanistan using Mastiff and Jackal alongside the usual kit.

The regimental cap-badge is the Austrian imperial coat of arms, a double-headed eagle, and their most famous ex-member is apparently Captain Mark Phillips, former husband of Princess Anne and father of Zara Phillips, the royal three-day eventer probably most famous for having a thing about rugby players, a tongue stud and a smaller vocabulary than her horse.

The Royal Scots Dragoon Guards (Carabiniers and Greys)

There's nothing not to like about the Royal Scots Dragoon Guards. They are desperately grand, and more than a few Eurotrash nobility have

The Times crossword: who would finish first?

featured among their officers over the years. They descend from the oldest line cavalry regiment in the Army; they were the first regiment to get the mighty Challie 2; they provide the armour punch in 7 Armoured Brigade, the British Army's premier heavy-metal shit-kicking formation; and they've had a number one hit single in the British pop charts. Gleaming!

As the name implies, the soldiers are recruited in Scotland – the SCOTS DG, to use their proper abbreviation, are the senior Scottish line regiment – while the officers are recruited mainly in the Scottish quarters of Knightsbridge, the King's Road and Monte Carlo.

Points to note about the SCOTS DG are that they have a pale grey, almost white beret which from a distance can easily be mistaken for the SAS sandy beret; they have a cool cap-badge featuring the French Napoleonic imperial eagle; and the Scots Greys, one of the regiments amalgamated into the SCOTS DG, were described in the film *Waterloo* as 'the noblest cavalry in all Europe . . . and the worst led'. The SCOTS DG are currently based in Fallingbostel ('Effing B'), not far from Hanover in northern Germany, but, like much of the rest of the Army, have recent tours in Iraq (and a squadron detachment to Afghanistan) under their belt.

The noblest cavalry in all Europe, and the worst led.

The Royal Dragoon Guards
The Skins; the Foreskins

The RDG is the result of the brutal amalgamation in 1993 of the 4th/7th Royal Dragoon Guards and the 5th Inniskilling Dragoon Guards (aka 'the Skins'). Both were regiments of Irish heritage and they still recruit some soldiers from Northern Ireland although most recruits now come from the north of England, and other traditional cavalry recruiting areas like Ghana and Fiji. Officers are the usual mixture.

The current role of the RDG is as the armoured regiment for 4 Armoured Brigade based in sunny Catterick, North Yorkshire, having moved there from Münster, Germany, in 2007. Their greatest triumph in recent years was the highly amusing 'Is This the Way to Armadillo' spoof video made while the RDG were on tour in Iraq.

Is this the way to armoured dildo?

The Queen's Royal Hussars

The QRH appeared, as if by magic, in 1993 as the result of the amalgamation of the Queen's Own Hussars (alias 'Queers on Horseback') and the Queen's Royal Irish Hussars.

The Irish traditions are maintained by the wearing of a rifle green beret, a dark green barrack dress jumper and the celebration of St Patrick's Day. Officers get to wear a nifty little item called a 'tent hat' (which comes from the QRIH) which is a green and gold tassled hat that looks like a cross

[LIVING THE ARMY LIFE] BOILING VESSEL

One of the most vital pieces of equipment in any armoured vehicle – a vessel for producing constant hot brews and food, and a very, very important advantage of an armoured over a light role battalion. 'BV Commander' is usually the first rank held in an armoured infantry battalion. The appointment is usually given on the new young soldier's first exercise. The young

Crow's face glows with pride when he is told he will be the Warrior's 'BV Commander' but drops when he finds out his duties are to keep the turret supplied with brews.

Where they got the 'tent hat' from.

between a Victorian gentleman's smoking cap and the kind of thing worn by Scott, Virgil and Alan Tracy in *Thunderbirds*. Other traditions include not drinking the loyal toast at mess dinners and not standing up for the National Anthem. Ooh er!

The most famous former member of the QRH is Winston Churchill, who was originally commissioned into the 4th Hussars in 1895 and acquired his taste for whisky and soda while serving with them in India. More recently, the QOH and QRIH have both produced a slack handful of senior steely-eyed Special Forces types fully capable of wreaking death and destruction while remaining impeccably gentlemanly.

The QRH currently fill the armoured role with 20 Armoured Brigade based in Sennelager, near Paderborn, Germany – home of Weltins lager and crucifying hangovers.

The 9th/12th Royal Lancers
The Delhi Spearmen; the Three Quarter Prancers; ¾ Popular

One of the older cavalry regiments, having not been amalgamated with anyone since 1960, the 9th/12th is the formation recce regiment for 7 Armoured Brigade based in Bergen-Höhne near Hanover. What kind of place is this? Well, the site of Belsen concentration camp is just across the road from the 7 Brigade garrison – definitely the kind of place where the most attractive sight is the road out.

The 9th/12th have a wide recruiting area, covering Derbyshire, Leicestershire, Northamptonshire, Rutland, Cambridgeshire, Bedfordshire, Hertfordshire, Essex and Greater London. According to one wise Arrser, 'Officers tend to be the usual cavalry types. Cavalry officers and Septics [Americans] tend to be very similar, they are either fucking liabilities or extremely good. The problem is that when you first meet them, you can't tell which category they fall into.'

The regiment's old and bold were famously wound up in the 1970s by a claim that, as Britain had joined the EU, their name would have to go decimal.

Cavalry modernization.

COMBAT VEHICLE

CHALLENGER 2 SPECIFICATION	
Function:	Main Battle Tank (MBT)
Weight:	62.5 tonnes
Length:	6.3m
Width:	3.5 m
Height:	2.49m
Crew:	4
Primary armament:	120mm L30 CHARM gun (50 rounds)
Secondary armament:	Co-axial 7.62 chaingun + 7.62 GPMG turret mount (4,000 rounds)
Maximum road speed:	56km/h
Engine:	Rolls-Royce CV12 Power 1200bhp
Range:	450km

CHALLENGER 2

Main Battle Tank of the British Army. Heavily armoured against rockets, mines and other tanks' shells, the Challenger 1 was dogged with problems and armed with the same L11A5 gun as used on the earlier Chieftain. The Challenger 2 is far superior and is armed with a more powerful L30A1 120mm main gun. A co-axial machine gun and mounting for a GPMG adds to the carnage potential.

The Challenger 2 is the most heavily protected tank in NATO, and thus the world. In operational service, only one has ever been destroyed, near Basra in 2003 as the result of a 'friendly fire' misidentification by the crew of another Challenger 2; and two have suffered serious damage from an RPG hit and from a roadside bomb with an explosively formed projectile. In another incident in Basra, a Challenger 2 survived a hit by a Milan guided missile and eight RPG warheads and was back in action within six hours; another tank survived over seventy RPG strikes. Not too shabby. And it has a BV for making brews!

The Challenger 2 is very likely to be the last MBT in the British armed forces as future trends suggest that armoured vehicles will be lighter and more agile, achieving protection through high-tech armour systems. It is unknown whether the Army will keep a reserve force of MBTs when the Challenger 2 is obsolete in case the world goes pear-shaped.

The King's Royal Hussars
The Emperor's Chambermaids; the Shitehawks; the Cherry Pickers

Formed at the end of 1992 from the Royal Hussars and the 14th/20th Hussars, the KRH have clung on to the crimson trousers and natty chocolate-brown beret of the Royal Hussars giving them a somewhat distinctive look. Cavalry officers are well known for wearing outrageous strides, but the KRH are the only ones with the balls to incorporate them into their uniform.

The regiment recruits soldiers from a wide geographical area including Buckinghamshire, Berkshire, Gloucestershire, Hampshire, Oxfordshire, Wiltshire, the Isle of Wight, the Channel Islands, Lancashire, Cumbria and Greater Manchester. Officers are recruited from such diverse locations as Eton, Winchester and Wellington.

The KRH are currently based in Tidworth – a garrison town on the edge of Salisbury Plain whose only claim to distinction is that it isn't Bulford – where they are the heavy armoured regiment for 12 Mechanized Brigade. It's worth noting that, on a good day with a following wind, it's possible to get from the Tidworth garrison guard room up the A303 and M3 and be on the King's Road in about seventy minutes. This might involve a bit of speeding, but it's worth it.

KRH officer selection.

The Light Dragoons
England's Northern Cavalry (yeah, right, but that's what they claim on their website); the Shite Dragoons

The LD recruit their soldiers from Tyneside and South Yorkshire and their officers from a selection of public schools of various degrees of poshness. They were created in 1992 from the original two 'vulgar fractions', the 13th/18th Hussars and the 15th/19th Hussars. They perform the formation recce role for 12 Mech Brigade and have been hard at it since the Balkans conflict kicked off in the early nineties, with deployments to the former Yugoslavia, Iraq and Afghanistan.

Having distinguished themselves on operations over an extended period, the LD were rewarded by being based at a former RAF base in Norfolk – proof, if any were required, that someone in the Ministry of Defence has both a warped sense of humour and a raging dislike of the Light Dragoons. The regimental website suggests that Swanton Morley is 'a stone's throw' from the bustling city of Norwich. It's highly likely, bearing in mind some of the pointy-headed retards who live in the area, that this description comes from personal experience.

The Queen's Royal Lancers
The Death or Glory Boys; the Boneheads

The QRL were formed in 1993 from the amalgamation of the 16th/5th Lancers and the 17th/21st Lancers. Their current role is providing formation recce for 19th Light Brigade, based out of Catterick, and they have undertaken recent deployments in both Iraq and Afghanistan.

The QRL will tell you that they're the best formation recce regiment in the Army, yadda yadda yadda. What they do have to shout about is one of the coolest cap-badges of any military regiment anywhere. In fact, the skull and crossbones 'motto' (as the 17th/21st used to call their cap-badge) is so cool that the 'Action Man British Army Officer' I got when I was seven years old was wearing one! The main recruiting area for the QRL is the East Midlands.

THE ROYAL TANK REGIMENT
The People's Cavalry; The Chavalry

The RTR are descended from the original unit that lumbered across no-man's land in Mark I tanks on the Western Front at Flers in September 1916. This subsequently became the Royal Tank Corps, and then in 1939 the Royal Tank Regiment. For reasons that are too trivial for anyone to care about, but which almost certainly relate to regimental snobbery, the regiments of line cavalry have never acted as 'parent' regiments (thus there have never been extra battalions of 'Royal Hussars' for example), whereas during World War Two the RTR was expanded enormously to well over twenty 'battalions'. After WW2 these were progressively reduced until 1993, when 1 RTR amalgamated with 4 RTR, and 2 RTR amalgamated with 3 RTR, becoming 1 and 2 RTR respectively. Easy, huh? I'm glad we got that settled.

1 RTR, which primarily recruits from Scotland and the north of England, now forms the core of the Joint CBRN Regiment based at RAF Honington (along with 27 Squadron RAF Regiment and two squadrons of TA Yeomanry). Their role is to detect, identify and monitor chemical, biological, radiological and nuclear threats to UK forces worldwide. In addition, one 1 RTR squadron is based at Warminster in a training and demonstration role, using Challie 2 and CVR(T), supporting training on Salisbury Plain and elsewhere.

2 RTR, which recruits from across England (the old 3 RTR were from the south-west and known as the 'Armoured Farmers' – oooh arr, oooh arr!), have a more traditional role, based in Aliwal Barracks, Tidworth. They provide the heavy armour punch for 1 Mech Brigade, the finest fighting brigade in all of Tidworth.

In days of yore, officers in the RTR tended to be serious, professional, middle-class types in comparison with the languid 'gentlemen' of the line cavalry. In reality this distinction disappeared long ago, although the prejudice never has. Perks of serving in the RTR include wearing attractive black coveralls, berets and jumpers (and mess kit if you're in the Sergeants' or Officers' Mess) – very SS.

[LIVING THE ARMY LIFE] BABIES' HEADS

1. (n) Tinned individual steak and kidney puddings issued in twenty-four-hour ration packs before the advent of 'boil in the bag' rations. These came with baked beans and tasted OK, but were primarily used on exercise for their amusement value as, when placed in a mess tin of water and heated, the tins would eventually detonate with spectacular effect, showering soldiers in the vicinity with hot fat, suet crust and some strange meat substitute.

2. (n) Tufts of earth and long grass to be found at Sennybridge, the Brecon Beacons, the Elan Valley and so on. These have been planted over many years by the staff of the Infantry Battle School at Brecon and 22 SAS Training Wing at Credenhill because they are no longer allowed to use live AP mines to fuck up their trainees' knees and ankles.

THE YEOMANRY

If you thought that was complicated, the TA bit of the Royal Armoured Corps is insanely complex. The Yeomanry regiments have been amalgamated so often that many components have become like a homeopathic remedy: diluted so much that no trace of the original material remains. Even more complicatedly, some parts of the Yeomanry have re-roled entirely, so that, for example, the Inns of Court and City Yeomanry, the Essex Yeomanry, the Berkshire Yeomanry, the County of London Yeomanry and various others are all now part of the TA Royal Signals, mostly as vestigial squadrons or troops; other Yeomanry 'regiments' are infantry, artillery, sappers, logistics, and even Army Air Corps units.

In the not too distant past, officers in the Yeomanry tended to be farmers, landowners, aristocrats and other country 'gentry', while the soldiers were the farm workers, gamekeepers, domestic staff and so on. The Officers' Messes of the Yeomanry could be very socially grand and, indeed, snobbish, after a bucolic fashion. By and large this has disappeared nowadays, not least because much of the landed aristocracy is busy either showing parties of day-trippers round their dilapidated houses or banging cocaine up their snouts by the shovel-load, machines have replaced farm workers, and domestic staff are Filipino and not eligible to join. Nowadays in the Yeomanry, country gentlemen are the exception rather than the norm and both officers and soldiers are much the same kind of people you find elsewhere in the TA.

There are three distinct roles for the RAC Yeomanry regiments: CBRN recce, Challenger 2 crew replacements and formation recce.

Cavalry and RTR: spot the difference.

The Royal Yeomanry

The RY's role is to provide reserve CBRN recce capability to augment the Joint CBRN Regiment and the existing regular formation recce regiments. There are five squadrons and a regimental band. The squadrons are:

A (Royal Wiltshire Yeomanry) Squadron in Swindon
B (Leicestershire and Derbyshire Yeomanry) Squadron in Leicester
C (Kent and Sharpshooters Yeomanry) Squadron in glamorous Croydon
S (Sherwood Rangers Yeomanry) Squadron in Nottingham
W (Westminster Dragoons) Squadron in London

Plus the Inns of Court and City Yeomanry Band in London. Regimental headquarters is also in Croydon.

Interestingly, having deployed a squadron on Op Telic 1, the RY is the only TA regiment since WW2 to have copped a battle honour: 'Iraq 2003'.

The Royal Wessex Yeomanry

The RWxY role is to train and supply crews and individual crew members for the Challenger 2 tanks used by the armoured regiments of the regular Army. In the modern world of high-tech weaponry it's much easier to break people than tanks so a few spares, properly trained and ready to go, are always a good idea.

The RWxY is organized into four squadrons (A Squadron does training and infrastructure, the rest provide the replacements):

A (Dorset Yeomanry) Squadron in Bovington
B (Royal Wiltshire Yeomanry) Squadron in Salisbury
C (Royal Gloucestershire Hussars) Squadron in Cirencester
D (Royal Devon Yeomanry) Squadron in Barnstaple

The Royal Mercian and Lancastrian Yeomanry

The RMLY are also an armoured replacement regiment. They have four squadrons plus a command troop and recce troop:

A (Staffordshire, Warwickshire and Worcestershire Yeomanry) Squadron in Dudley
B (Shropshire Yeomanry) Squadron in Telford
C (Cheshire Yeomanry) Squadron in Chester
D (Duke of Lancaster's Own Yeomanry) Squadron in Wigan
H (Herefordshire Light Infantry) Detachment in Hereford

The RMLY is one of two Yeomanry regiments that have billionaire Major General the Duke of Westminster as their Honorary Colonel. All the officers always refer to him as 'Gerald Westminster' in order to suggest they're on first-name terms with him. As it happens, he's such a nice bloke they probably are!

The Queen's Own Yeomanry

The QOY is the only formation recce regiment in the TA equipped with CVR(T). They are based in Scotland, Northern Ireland and the north-east of England and reinforce the regular formation recce regiments:

A (Ayrshire Yeomanry) Squadron based in Ayr and Motherwell (who wear the light-grey beret of the Scots DG)
B (North Irish Horse) Squadron based in Belfast
C (Fife and Forfar Yeomanry/Scottish Horse) Squadron based at Cupar and Forfar
D (Northumberland Hussars) Squadron based at Newcastle and Sunderland
Y (Yorkshire Yeomanry) Squadron in York and Hull

[LIVING THE ARMY LIFE] DRUG CASES

Mostly drug cases don't go through the court-martial system or Colchester these days. Those who get caught by the CDT (Compulsory Drug Testing) teams are faced with an administrative discharge from the Army straight away. Some argue that this is an unrealistic approach, given the prevalence of drug abuse among young people from all parts of society, but it's hard to see how the Army can do otherwise.

There are stories around that some disaffected service personnel are deliberately playing the system, trying to second-guess when the CDT team will visit their unit – it's often after a block leave or overseas training exercise – and either timing drug abuse to try to leave a long-enough gap so they don't get detected, or deliberately taking drugs so they get caught and discharged. Both cunning plans have the potential to drop you in the shit. Getting rifted out of the Army for drug abuse is not guaranteed to impress future employers, unless you plan on working for the Medellín cocaine cartel.

COMBAT VEHICLE, RECONNAISSANCE (TRACKED)

CVR(T)

Basically an 8-ton tracked MG Midget on steroids with either a turret or not, the CVR(T) can move like a fat girl towards the last bun when properly maintained. Rumour has it that the designer of the final drive went insane trying to figure out how he actually made it work, as they feature epicyclic gears (known to the VMs as epileptic gears). With all the new anti-mine gubbins fitted for Iraq and Afghanistan it now weighs in the region of 14 tons.

Variants

The initial prototype looked like a four-year-old's drawing of a tank. Alvis developed multiple models from the basic design, including

- FV101 Scorpion (76mm turret) (now obsolete)
- FV107 Scimitar (30mm cannon turret)
- FV106 Samson (REME recovery variant)
- FV105 Sultan (Command vehicle)
- FV104 Samaritan (armoured ambulance)

as well as
- FV103 Spartan (mini APC beloved of assault troops everywhere)

which formed the basis for a range of carriers, including

- FV102 Striker (Swingfire anti-tank missile launcher)
- FV108 Streaker (LAD variant)
- FV120 Spartan MCT (with Milan Compact Turret) and Stormer (supersized Spartan – apparently quite good, so never bought in quantity)

and was also the basis for the Shielder mine-laying vehicle. The Sabre is the Scorpion fitted with the old Fox CVR(W) turret.

All had the Jaguar 4.2 petrol engine (derated) initially, but most if not all of the in-service fleet was converted to Cummins diesel power during mid-life improvement updates from the mid-eighties onwards. The Jag engine meant that the CVR(T) vehicles could easily do 50mph on a good road.

Armament

The 76mm gun in the Scorpion was a development of a weapon originally developed for gunboats. On exercise it fired blank rounds which, while impressively noisy in themselves, could be tuned up by the addition of an opened can of compo boiled sweets: Johnny Highlander may be a doughty fighter in a corner, but he won't face molten hard candy flying at him at Mach 5 from fifty yards away.

The 30mm Rarden cannon of the Scimitar and Sabre is a manual-loading clip-fed design developed by the Royal Armament Research and Development Establishment Enfield (yes, I know it should have been Rardee, but that would have sounded silly). Rarden has a very flat trajectory with a high muzzle velocity, and a skilled gunner/commander team can put six rounds on target in as much time as it takes to think it. It fires a variety of ammunition including HE, some form of AP Sabot, and possibly still APSE (Armour-Piercing Smoke-Ejecting, or Special Effects, take your choice), which was just a polite way to get white phosphorus into the other guy's turret and ruin his afternoon without trampling over the Geneva Convention.

The Future

No further variants are planned as the MoD have run out of names starting with 'S'. You can buy a delivery mileage only, off-the-shelf, NATO reserve stock Spartan for £7,500 from Witham Specialist Vehicles in Lincolnshire. Worth thinking about to beat that commute?

RECRUITMENT

The basic prerequisites for joining the British Army fall into three categories: age, qualifications, and physical condition.

AGE

Between sixteen and thirty-three years old. Under eighteens need the consent of their parent or guardian; older people with professional or specialist qualifications can be considered. Ghastly lefties have attempted to claim that the British Army recruits 'child soldiers'. The reality is that soldiers under the age of eighteen don't go into combat, they are trainees. It's simply an attempt to make it look like the British Army kidnaps kids from their families, transports them to 'Camp Beaucoup Kill-Kill Numbah Ten' in the jungle, gets them strung out on smack and then sends them out to rape nuns. This is rarely the case.

QUALIFICATIONS

Depends on trade. Some require no specific qualifications other than a basic level of literacy and numeracy, others require specific GCSEs or equivalent.

PHYSICAL CONDITION

Candidates need to be healthy enough to pass a full Army medical. Initial sifting is done on the basis of a questionnaire sent to a candidate's GP. Those with a range of chronic and acute health problems may be automatically rejected. Such problems include:

Chest Disorders

>> Asthma, wheeze or asthma symptoms (and treatment) during the previous four years.

>> Chronic lung diseases (e.g. emphysema, bronchiectasis and cystic fibrosis).

>> Active tuberculosis (TB).

Back Problems

>> Spinal surgery (including internal fixation or fusion). Recurrent lower back pain. Spina bifida.

Bone or Joint Problems

» Meniscectomy (knee cartilage operation) within the last year. Surgical repair of a knee cruciate ligament. Lower limb fractures with internal fixation (metalwork) still in place.

Loss of a limb

» Complete loss of a thumb. Total loss of either great toe. Any degree of club foot (including past surgery). Chronic joint diseases (e.g. ankylosing spondylitis, psoriatic arthritis, rheumatoid arthritis and gout). Reiter's disease in last five years. Osteochondritis dissecans.

Eye Disorders

» Chronic eye diseases (e.g. glaucoma, keratoconus and retinitis pigmentosa or extreme colour blindness). Squint surgery in last six months. Corneal problems (e.g. corneal graft and re-current corneal ulcers). Loss or dislocation of eye lens. Cataract or cataract surgery. Detached retina.

Ear Disorders

» Presence of eardrum ventilation tubes or grommets. Current perforation of ear drum. Chronic ear diseases (e.g. cholesteatoma).

Abdominal Problems

» Chronic abdominal diseases. Kidney disorders. Donation of a kidney in last two years. Kidney disease in last two years.

Neurological Disorders

» Epilepsy or more than one seizure/fit after the age of five.
» Single seizure/fit in the last four years.
» Multiple sclerosis.

Skin Problems

» Malignant melanoma or skin cancer within two years. Active skin disease (e.g. eczema and widespread psoriasis).

Pregnancy

» Current pregnancy or childbirth in the last six months.

Chronic Blood Disease

» Sickle cell disease. Congenital spherocytosis. Thalassaemia. HIV seropositivity/AIDS. Carriers of hepatitis B or C. Past history of leukaemia or malignant lymphoma.

Psychiatric Problems

» Schizophrenia. Obsessive-compulsive disorder. Alcohol or drug dependence. Post-traumatic stress disorder.

Other Conditions

» Loss of spleen (splenectomy).

» Transplanted organs.

Faster, pussy-cat. Kill, kill!

>> Severe allergic reactions and/or anaphylaxis requiring adrenalin injection precautions (e.g. nut allergy).

>> Circulation problems (e.g. Raynaud's disease).

>> Diabetes.

>> Diseases (e.g. glandular or hormonal) requiring long-term medication or replacement therapy.

In terms of general fitness, you don't need to be an Olympic athlete, but at the Army Selection Centre you will be expected to do a 1.5-mile run in a given time as well as a series of other physical tests. You will be graded on this and, for example, anyone going slower than nine minutes forty seconds won't be considered for the Parachute Regiment. So get fit! Start running, go to a gym,

take a class at your local leisure centre, play five-a-side footie, use a bicycle: anything that will get your muscles working and your heart pumping.

FIRST STEPS

The first thing to do is a bit of background research. You can fill out the 'Army Interest' forms online or you can pop along to your local recruiting office and make contact directly with the recruiting team.

This is what will follow:

INITIAL VISIT

If you've filled out a form online or phoned the call centre you'll eventually receive an invitation to a recruiting office. You can also turn up on spec. This is an interview to see how interested you are, and whether there are any obvious things, like your franchised heroin dealership or the FUCK OFF! tattoo on your forehead, which might rule you out. If you haven't already done it, you'll be asked to fill out a basic questionnaire so that you can be invited back for a formal interview. If you have, you may get your first formal interview there and then.

INTERVIEW 1

The first formal interview is to check the information provided on the application form and to ensure that you have your parents' permission if under eighteen. You will then be booked to do the BARB and 'Basic Skills' tests, or you may be able to do them there and then. These are basic aptitude tests that determine which trades you will be eligible for. With the BARB test completed you can make three choices from the jobs available to you, and then you get invited back for the next stage.

INTERVIEW 2

The second interview is a formal assessment of your suitability, after which the recruiter will make a recommendation as to whether you should be accepted or not. He or she will ask you a wide range of questions about your background, achievements and aspirations, and about your reasons for your three job choices.

INTERVIEW 3

The third and final interview before the ADSC will be with a senior recruiter who will use the information provided by you at the previous interviews and test results to confirm the recruiter's recommendation. It will cover some of the same ground as previous interviews but will concentrate on your readiness to go forward with the selection process. At the end, the interviewer will tell you whether you can go on to ADSC or not.

ADSC

The four ADSCs – in Pirbright, Lichfield, Edinburgh and Belfast – are where the two-day selection process takes place. The key events in this are a full Army medical examination, a fitness assessment, some team and individual tasks, the Technical Selection Test for those going into technical trades, a further interview, a two-minute 'ice-breaker' talk about yourself to the group, and lectures and presentations from the staff. If you get through all this, well done, you're on your way; if not, you'll get advice about what you can do next. Some fails are real showstoppers, others will require you to delay your application for a set period until, say, an injury has had more chance to heal. Even if you do fail, at least you've had a go at joining the best army in the world. It isn't for everyone. Many are called, rather fewer are chosen.

A RECRUITER WRITES . . .

A recruiter: don't be fooled!

The first time you rock up at the Armed Forces Careers Information Office you are actually at your first interview; you aren't told this, but it's true. Dress smartly. A jacket and tie wouldn't go amiss, but at least wear clean clothes, jeans or trousers without rips, and don't wear baseball caps or hats as this will hide your face on the camera you are looking at when you are buzzed in. Turn off your mobile phones, iPods, laptops or whatever other electrical equipment you are carrying. If anything goes off mid-interview, that's a schoolboy error on your part.

The recruiter is not your mate, friend, bezzer or buddy. They don't expect you to leap to attention or kiss their arse, but understand that they are relatively senior members of the organization you are trying to join. They will tell you their first name when they introduce themselves, so use that (they will be using your first name).

It's a good idea to have done some research on the Army Jobs website before you go so that you can tell the recruiter which ones you're interested in, but if you don't have the time or the access the recruiter will spend part of this first interview going through options with you. Pay attention to what he or she is saying. Don't sit there staring out of the window or yawning because you will be marked down as a time-waster.

When filling in the initial contact form try to make it neat and make sure you put a valid phone number, address and/or postcode, as well as your date of birth.

The recruiter may want to check your height and weight (so wear clean socks!) but you will certainly be asked the 'Big Four' questions, on criminal records, debts, drugs and tattoos.

Crime

If you have more than two unspent convictions of any kind, special permission will be required for you to join. If you have been sentenced to more than thirty months in prison or have been convicted for possession with intent to supply you will be barred from joining. If you are banned due to drink-driving you will only have a choice of four jobs.

Debt

Too much will prevent you from joining: the rule is no more than 25 to 30 per cent of your income should be going out in repayments.

Drugs

If you are a habitual user of illegal drugs or have any convictions for supplying, you will be barred from entry.

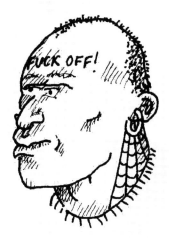

Tattoos

Any that are sexist, racist or likely to offend will also be a bar to entry.

Facial tattoos: just say no.

Medical criteria are examined on a case-by-case basis. However, what will stop you is if you have been issued with an inhaler for asthma in the past four years, you've taken ADHD or ADD medication in the past three years, or you've self-harmed (in which case we are not going to give you automatic weapons).

If you are an overseas candidate (i.e. not from the UK or Irish Republic) you must have at least four years left on your passport and at least four months on your visa.

Once you get through all that you will be invited to attend a BARB test (that's 'British Army Recruiting Battery' to you) at a time and date of your convenience. We work around you. You should get a DVD with all the jobs on it. Watch it. Note down any jobs that jump out at you and if they come up on your job list, job done. You will need three job choices. If you qualify at ADSC for all three you are offered all three; if you don't make job one you are offered two and three; if you don't make jobs one and two you are offered job three. So don't pluck one out of the air for jobs two or three as you may end up only being offered these.

When you arrive for your BARB, arrive early, as all of your paperwork needs checking prior to you sitting the test.

Make sure you have filled in the AFCO 4 (application form) completely; areas commonly missed are religion, under-care order section, referees, next of kin and GP details. Check it before coming, then check it again. Make sure you have signed it, or if you are under eighteen make sure a parent/guardian has signed it. Make sure you bring with you and have signed the tattoo sheet and crime sheet. Make sure you have ID: the minimum is a birth certificate; if you have a driving licence make sure it is both parts; if you have a passport make sure it's in date. If you have changed your name, make sure you bring with you your change of name deed. If you are claiming any GCSEs or equivalent, make sure you bring the certificates. GCSE grades D and above will give you some good jobs but Cs are better in English Language, Mathematics and Sciences.

When you sit the BARB it is all about speed and accuracy. Your gut instinct is usually right, so if you don't know it hit one and move on. If it is fifty-fifty you may get it right. People who sit there taking their time and get them all right will have a poor score that's down to speed. If you get a bad score all is not lost as you can sit the BARB three times in a year with a twenty-eight-day break in between.

The jobs range from 26 to 60. The average is 50, and you will be told whether you have scored below or above average. The assessment lasts forty-five minutes for each one; I have seen it done in fifteen with a level 2.

Once the test is done you will be given your job list and your recruiter will go through each job with a brief description of each one. You can ask for as many job briefs to be printed as you want, or you can research on the net (Army Jobs).

The job brief contains mountains of information. The minimum we are after is where you are going for phase 1 and 2 training, how long is training, and what will you learn, which is such things as living in the field, how to handle and fire a weapon, and how to tackle an assault course. You need to know this for all three of your job choices.

I always tell my candidates to look at the bigger picture. If you only do four years minimum what are you going to do when you get out? If you want to work for Gordon Ramsay one day, don't become a bricklayer. If you are unsure about what you want to do, ask about 'Look at Life' courses. These are five days long and you get to see what your job entails. The course is free, your train tickets will be booked by your recruiter, we feed you, accommodate you and get you home. You will not be able to drink and you will be treated as a soldier.

If you want to join the Parachute Regiment, get yourself on one of their 'Look at Life' weekends. You can do this direct via the web or ask your recruiter for a number. They will send you train tickets direct. If you get a green light from them you should do well at PRAC, if they tell you don't bother, then don't; if they tell you to do some more work on your fitness, do it.

You will have your RG8 medical form explained to you and how to fill it in; make sure you complete every question. The first page will contain your height, weight and BMI, if you are JE or SE, and what selection centre you will be going to. The next page is blank. The first page you need to mark has your name and address at the top – make sure it is correct (make sure the information you gave the recruiter was correct). It asks if you have ever applied to join before: if you have and have filled in a previous RG8, tick yes; if you only picked up a magazine, tick no; if you have ticked yes but didn't go anywhere with it you will delay your application as people will be chasing your previous docs.

The next page deals with your eyesight. If you have been prescribed glasses or contacts tell your recruiter as you will need a separate optician's report. Take this anywhere you can get a free eye test and make sure they put the information on this form; if you walk away and it's not on our form you will delay your application as you will have to go back and get the information on one of our forms.

When it asks if you do or do not wish to have access to your medical report I would put 'do not wish' as then your doctor will sign your form; if you put yes you may have to pay them yourself. You do not need to see your report at this stage (or any stage come to think of it). If you are underage make sure your parents/guardians sign it.

Now you have to fill in every question. Miss one out and the form comes back for you to do it again, delaying your application. When it asks what physical activity you do, make sure you put something.

Once you get to page 10 you are done. Take it to your doctor for verification. Once this is done it will be sent back to your office for delivery to your selection centre. The medical staff review your form there and hopefully it will come back as suitable to attend selection. Further information may be required; if so, they may contact your GP direct or send you a letter telling you what they need. Do whatever it asks in a timely manner or you will only delay your application. You may get a deferral – again, a letter will be sent to you telling you why and how long your deferral period is. You may get a rejection. Your recruiter will not know what further information is required, why you are deferred or why you are rejected – it is all in confidence.

The bottom line for the whole process is this: make sure you've filled everything out and answered every question accurately. Fail to do that and you delay your application. And if you're asked for further information, make sure you supply it as soon as possible.

Also, be realistic. If you aren't fit, you can't join the Paras or the infantry. If you haven't got any qualifications, they aren't going to make you a radar tech. Treat the whole process like you would any other job interview, and you won't go far wrong.

INFANTRY

Grunts.

Moving on from the people who ride to war in large and heavy concoctions of armour plate, firepower and machinery, we now come to the infantry, many of whom also now go to war in large and heavy concoctions of armour plate, firepower and machinery. Nevertheless, despite all the improvements in technology, the modern infantryman in the twenty-first-century British Army is still doing a job that would be recognizable to his counterparts from 250 years ago, and still whingeing about it just as much.

There are four basic types of infantry in the British Army, plus the TA Infantry.

1 Armoured Infantry Armoured infantry use the Warrior IFV as their main equipment. This is a chunky 25-ton armoured personnel carrier with a 30mm cannon (which can knock out soft-skin vehicles, lightly armoured vehicles and defensive positions, but not tanks) which carries a section of seven fully equipped soldiers plus a crew of three for the vehicle (commander, gunner and driver). Critically, it also includes a boiling vessel, giving its passengers and crew the ability to make tea and coffee at will without fucking around with mess-tins and hexy. The basic concept of armoured infantry is

that they are fast-moving and well protected, able to operate in close co-operation with the heavy armour Challenger 2 regiments of the RAC, with whom they are grouped in armoured and mech brigades.

2 Mechanized Infantry If we are being completely honest, 'mech inf' are a kind of poor man's version of armoured infantry. For the last twenty-six years their main equipment has been the Saxon wheeled APC. This was designed for the days of the Cold War when the plan was for large numbers of infantrymen to deploy by road from the UK to Germany, to stem the approaching Soviet hordes. The Saxon is basically a four-wheel-drive truck with sufficient armour plate to protect its occupants from light fragmentation and small-arms fire. It would have been much quicker than using tracked APCs to get units into position, but its off-road performance is pretty dreadful: it's wheeled, heavy (at 10 tons), and top heavy too. It isn't a vehicle for fighting in, but then again, it wasn't designed to be.

Anyway, the Saxon is now being replaced with the 'new' Bulldog tracked APC. The Bulldog gets the inverted commas round 'new' because it is actually nearly fifty years old, being an upgrade of the old FV 432 APC which was introduced in 1963 (the last new one was delivered in 1971). To be fair, they have been substantially upgraded, with a new engine system as well as air-con and reactive armour for use in Afghanistan. Again, it isn't a vehicle to fight from like the Warrior is, but something which will get the infantryman close to the battlefield with a reasonable degree of protection.

The Bulldog: you may not be able to polish a turd, but you can try.

3 Light Role Infantry Light role infantry don't get armoured vehicles at all. They are moved around in trucks, Land Rovers of various sorts, helicopters and on foot. In general war, light role battalions are likely to find themselves involved in tasks such as route proving and security, securing brigade and divisional supply areas, guarding PoWs, and so on. They might also find themselves being used in specialized roles, like jungle warfare. In peacetime, several of the light role battalions do ceremonial and public-duties tasks. In addition, two light role infantry battalions are committed to the air assault role with 16 Air Assault Brigade, and one battalion is committed to 3 Commando Brigade.

4 Air Assault Infantry The final infantry role is air assault. Two of the three battalions of the Parachute Regiment do this full time (1 Para is now acting as the core unit of the 'Special Forces Support Group') and three light role line infantry battalions rotate through the role (two at any one time). The UK converted its Airborne Brigade into a primarily helicopter-mounted Air Assault Brigade in 1999, partly in recognition of the reality that large-scale parachute operations are a thing of the past, but mostly in order to incorporate the astonishing mobility and firepower of the Apache helicopter into a manoeuvre formation.

5 TA Infantry The fourteen battalions of TA infantry are primarily now used to provide reinforcements and incremental personnel at all ranks for their associated regular battalions deploying on operations. The largest

Apache ... grrrr, sexy!

groupings recently deployed have been companies formed for force protection operations; more usually, TA infantry personnel are slotted into regular units as individuals.

In the dim and distant past, infantry units were usually formed in localized areas by wealthy men who would then command them in the service of the Crown. The link between localities and 'their' regiments became concrete in the eighteenth century, and formalized by the Cardwell Reforms in the 1860s. Sadly, in more recent years cuts in funding, and thus amalgamations, have served to dilute and undermine local connections. They do still exist, but they are neither as strong nor as localized as they used to be. For some years most of the individual regiments had been grouped into administrative 'divisions' (e.g. the Guards Division, the King's Division, the Light Division, the Scottish Division, and so on) but these have been partly superseded by the creation of 'large regiments' which have grouped together the older single-battalion regiments into larger administrative units within which personnel can be cross-posted to ensure they get sufficient breadth and variety in their careers.

THE FOOT GUARDS

The Woodentops; the Marbletops

The origin of the Guards was as elite infantry recruited and organized to be a personal military force for the British monarch. This bodyguard role is still reflected to some extent in the modern Guards regiments which provide the majority of public-duties and ceremonial troops to guard Buckingham Palace, the Tower of London and Windsor Castle.

In the past the elite status of the Guards was derived from their rigorous training and fierce discipline, but things have subtly changed over the years and their 'eliteness' is now largely derived from their social status and their position of influence within the British Army. This doesn't mean that the Guards have declined in quality as soldiers: they seem to produce nearly as many successful SAS officers and soldiers as the Paras, and in fact Guards recruits do a slightly extended basic Combat Infantry Course (CIC) in comparison to most other parts of the infantry to accommodate extra training in drill for the ceremonial part of their role. It's an undeniable fact that anyone who has served in the Guards can be relied on to polish their boots and shoes to perfection for the rest of their lives.

Now, in a modern democracy like ours, where we even had a socialist government for thirteen years, being in cahoots with the royal family and the monarchy shouldn't matter . . . but somehow it does.

Kweeeeeeeeek ... MUNK! Duff-dite-duff-dite ...

Where almost every other infantry regiment in the British Army has been merged and amalgamated up the wazoo, somehow the Guards have managed to get through more or less unscathed. True, the Grenadiers, Coldstream and Scots Guards lost their second battalions, but they weren't disbanded, just made 'dormant' (whatever that means), and in fact kept going in the form of incremental public-duties companies. It's true that Chelsea Barracks has been flogged off to property developers, but the public-duties companies got moved to Woolwich instead, swapping a nasty sixties glass-and-concrete monstrosity for one of the most beautiful buildings in London. Oh, the hardship! How have they managed this feat of survival? Well, being in touch with the Queen and other senior members of the royal family on a day-to-day basis hasn't done any harm. If you want someone to put in a good word for you, the Head of State is a good starting point. This is reciprocated: service in the Guards as an officer or NCO/Warrant Officer is a good stepping-stone for a future career at court.

One of the most enduring myths about the Guards is that you need to be an uber-posh Hooray Henry to become an officer. Although you will come across some extremely grand Guards officers they are no longer all, or even mostly, like this. In part this is because the Guards no longer apply their own filter to potential officers. Up until the early 1990s the Guards ran 'Brigade Squad', a six-week beasting session for officer applicants which gave the regiments a chance to run their eye over candidates and get rid of any they didn't like. In theory this was fine; in practice it tended to mean that officers were drawn from a narrow stereotype. Nowadays the Guards select their officers on the same basis as the rest of the Army: performance at Sandhurst. Family connections help, but only in the same way that they do with other regiments, and it's a much more transparent process. Among the current crop of Guards officers, a lot seem to be the sons of officers from other parts of the Army.

A special feature of the Guards is that they have managed to retain their stranglehold on Sandhurst. The Academy Sergeant Major, the College RSMs and the Company Sergeant Majors are Guardsmen, as are a good number of the platoon Colour Sergeants. This helps to ensure that the British Army

WARRIOR FV510 SPECIFICATION	
Function:	Infantry Fighting Vehicle (IFV)
Weight:	25.4 tonnes
Length:	6.3m
Width:	3.03m
Height:	2.8m
Crew:	3 (commander, gunner, driver) + 7 troops
Primary armament:	30mm L21A1 Rarden cannon
Secondary armament:	L94A1 co-axial 7.62mm chaingun
Speed:	46mph (75km/h)
Engine:	Perkins V8 Condor 550hp (410kW)

THE WARRIOR (FV510)

The Warrior (FV510) is an IFV designed to carry seven troops under armour to an objective and give them firepower support when they have disembarked. It has the firepower, speed and manoeuvrability to keep up with and support Challenger 2 MBTs. It replaced the FV430 series of APCs. While not as well armed as the US Bradley IFV (the Bradley's 25mm chaingun is believed to have destroyed Iraqi T-72 tanks at close range), it is better protected, although weak under-armour has been highlighted after several Warriors were destroyed in Afghanistan by mines.

That's the reality. The perception is that it's a great big thrumming beast of a thing with a big growly engine and full of blokes who, when not asleep or having a wank in the driver's compartment, are the best infantry in the world. Goes really quick anywhere you want to take it, and stops bloody sharpish too.

To compensate for its speed, presence and protection it is equipped with comedy weapons that need precognitive abilities ('I think I'll need HE in three rounds' time . . .'), or, when using the chaingun, a patient, co-operative and slow-moving enemy. A typical engagement sequence is as follows: 'Firing now!' BANG! . . . clunk. 'Stoppage . . . feck, hang on a bit – bollocks, dropped the spinny thing . . . feck . . . oh, they've gone . . .'

officer of the twenty-first century can stamp his (or her) feet and polish his toecaps as effectively as his predecessors.

The bottom line, according to a friend of mine who was a notably rebellious Guards officer, is that the Guards are all about tradition and doing things in a traditional way. If, as an officer or soldier, that's what floats your boat, you'll fit in fine. This can be good and bad: the Guards remained effectively 'whites only' until the 1990s and they didn't start accepting black and other ethnic minority recruits without a struggle, which was bitter at times. Thankfully this seems to have been resolved now and it isn't unusual to see a black face under a bearskin or slashed peak cap. At the end of the day, they do do things differently to the rest of the Army – for example, Corporals in the Guards are called Lance Sergeants and are members of the Sergeants' Mess – but it keeps them happy and out of everyone else's hair, which can only be a good thing.

Beret: *khaki with blue and red flash behind regimental badge.*
Stable belt: *blue and red.*

The Grenadier Guards
The Bill Browns; the Dandies
The senior, although not the oldest, Guards regiment is the Grenadiers. Currently based at Wellington Barracks, just across the road from Buckingham Palace, they combine the ceremonial public-duties role with being a light role infantry battalion.

The Grenadiers recruit from across England. When not polishing their boots, stamping their feet and lining the gutters of Whitehall and the Mall in honour of the deputy Prime Minister of Outer Slovakistan, they can be found in such desirable locales as Sangin and Musa Qala.

The Coldstream Guards
The Lilywhites; the Sheep-shaggers
The Coldstream Guards is the oldest continuously serving regiment in the British Army, having originally been formed as part of Cromwell's New Model Army in 1650. They are currently a light role infantry battalion based in Aldershot and will, in the long term, alternate with the Irish Guards in performing public duties and deploying to such desirable holiday locations as Helmand Province.

The Coldstream recruit from the areas they passed through during their march from Coldstream, in the Scottish borders, to London after their formation.

The Scots Guards
The Jocks
Unlike the rest of the Guards who are programmed to alternate between light role and ceremonial public duties for the foreseeable future, the Jocks have

got the gig as the armoured infantry battalion in 4 Mech Brigade, based in Catterick, having relocated from Münster in Germany a couple of years ago.

Most of the Scots accents in the Officers' Mess belong to the LE officers; the DE officers, who are actually Scots, are generally posh enough to make Brian Sewell sound a bit common.

The Irish Guards
The Micks

Traditionally, the Irish Guards has been the regiment with the largest number of Catholic officers and soldiers from the Irish Republic, although nowadays there are larger numbers from the north of Ireland, and indeed many 'ethnic Irish' from England and Scotland. Even so, in the interests of regimental harmony the Micks never deployed to Ulster during Op Banner. Nowadays they are a light role battalion based at Windsor, alternating in the public-duties role with the Coldstream.

Traditionally the Micks were officered by grand Anglo-Irish families from north and south of the border, but nowadays you will hear the odd Irish accent in their very friendly Officers' Mess.

The Welsh Guards
The Taffs

The junior regiment of Foot Guards is the Welsh Guards, raised during the First World War and, surprisingly enough, recruited almost entirely in Wales (although, as usual, the officers tend to be upper-middle-class Englishmen with Welsh connections rather than full-on sheep molesters). They are now based at Lille Barracks in Aldershot alternating between light role infantry and public duties with the Grenadiers.

During their 2009 tour in Afghanistan, the Welsh Guards sadly lost their Commanding Officer, Lt Col Rupert Thorneloe, killed by an IED – the highest-ranking British officer to be killed in action since Lt Col H. Jones VC during the Falklands War. Lt Col Thorneloe was one of five members of the battlegroup killed during that deployment.

The London Regiment

The Guards don't have a TA regiment as such, but they are affiliated with the Londons, who wear the Guards' blue and red tactical recognition flash. The Londons are divided into an HQ Company and four rifle companies that are located at various TA centres across London and which wear the head-dress and cap-badge of their 'parent' units:

A (London Scottish) Company

B (Queen's Regiment) Company
C (City of London Fusiliers) Company
D (London Irish Rifles) Company

THE ROYAL REGIMENT OF SCOTLAND

The creation of the Royal Regiment of Scotland in 2006 was highly controversial both inside and outside the Army. It was driven by a strong desire to achieve cost-cutting through economies of scale and by the sad reality that several of the Scottish infantry regiments were having real problems recruiting in their traditional areas and were being forced to rely increasingly on Commonwealth recruits, particularly from Fiji and southern Africa, to make up the numbers. The fact that it happened during a period when the British Army was involved in two high-intensity campaigns in Iraq and Afghanistan, with the Black Watch deployed in a high-threat area supporting the US Army, only heightened the controversy and the bitterness it caused. Another factor was that the then CGS, General Sir Mike Jackson – aka The Prince of Darkness – delegated the decision on how the six regular Scottish line battalions would be reduced to five to the 'Council of Scottish Colonels', who decided to amalgamate the Royal Scots with the King's Own Scottish Borderers, much against the wishes of the KOSB. Uniquely among the 'new' large infantry regiments, the Scots have retained the identities of previous regiments as far as possible in their regimental titles.

Head-dress: khaki tam o'shanter with regimental hackle.
Stable belt: tartan.
Tartan: Government 1A (a version of the Black Watch tartan).

The Royal Scottish Borderers, 1 Scots

The Royal Scottish Borderers recruit in Dumfries and Galloway, the Lothians, Edinburgh, the Borders and Galloway. It was formed from the Royal Scots ('Pontius Pilate's Bodyguard'), hitherto the oldest line infantry regiment in the British Army, and the KOSB, aka 'the Bing Crosbies', which also dated from the seventeenth century. Both battalions had issues with recruiting sufficient soldiers from their home area and had been chronically under-strength, taking augmentees from other regiments for operations. They are a light role infantry battalion, assigned to 19 Light Brigade and based in Edinburgh.

Regimental hackle: black.

The Royal Highland Fusiliers, 2 Scots
The Weegies; the Jimmy-Jimmy Fuck-Fucks

The RHF recruit terrifying Glaswegian Neds and turn them into terrifying

Glaswegian soldiers. When not biting the heads off live grizzly bears they are a light role/public-duties battalion based in Penicuik, near Edinburgh. By contrast with the soldiers, RHF officers tend to be rather civilized and pukka; David Niven served in the Highland Light Infantry, one of the two predecessor regiments of the RHF. Fearless in battle and in bars worldwide and renowned for their prowess in the black arts (thievery, smuggling and general lawlessness), they see themselves as fun-sized shock troops, stormtroopers in miniature. Terry Pratchett's 'Nac Mac Feegles' are loosely based on the RHF. They love nothing more than to fight and steal. If no OPFOR is available they will turn on neighbouring troops; if that fails, they will turn on each other.

Never discuss football or religion: the entire battalion supports either Rangers or Celtic/Ian Paisley or the Pope. And never leave your kit unattended.

Regimental hackle: white.

Typical RHF soldier ... Note white 'hackle'.

The Black Watch, 3 Scots
The Black Death; the Jock Watch

One of the most famous regimental names in the British Army, whose tartan is made into mini-skirts and wrapped around the haunches of nubile teenagers worldwide. The regiment recruits its soldiers from Fife, Dundee, Angus, Perth and Kinross and is a light role infantry battalion subordinate to 19 Light Brigade and based at Fort George, Inverness. Until the formation of the Royal Regiment of Scotland in 2006, the Black Watch didn't wear a cap-badge on their tam o'shanters.

Regimental hackle: red.

The Highlanders, 4 Scots
Variations on sheep-shagging

The Highlanders are the result of the amalgamation in 1994 of the Queen's Own Highlanders and the Gordons, becoming part of the Royal Regiment of Scotland in 2006. They are currently based in Fallingbostel, Germany as the armoured infantry battlegroup of 7 Armoured Brigade. Soldiers are recruited from the Highlands and islands of the north of Scotland; officers are typically a mix of Scots and Anglo-Scots.

Regimental hackle: *blue.*

The Argyll and Sutherland Highlanders, 5 Scots
The Argyll and Bolton Wanderers

Recruited, as one might expect, from the Highlands of Argyll and Sutherland. Before their incorporation into the Scots, the Argylls got to wear natty pale-blue shirts and jumpers, together with their dashing kilts. Over the years the regiment has had something of a charmed life, surviving attempts to amalgamate it on several previous occasions. It is now in the light/air assault role as part of 16 Air Assault Brigade, based in Canterbury.

Regimental hackle: *green.*

52nd Lowland, 6 Scots

52nd Lowland are a TA battalion recruited from southern Scotland and the Borders, and thus affiliated with 1 and 2 Scots, whose black and white hackles they wear, depending on company location.

Argyll and Sutherland Highlanders Wives Club picnic.

51st Highland, 7 Scots

51st Highland are a TA battalion recruited throughout the Highland regions of Scotland and associated with 3, 4 and 5 Scots, depending on location.

THE DUKE OF LANCASTER'S REGIMENT

The Duke of Lancaster's Regiment (Lancs) was formed in 2006 by the merger of the three north-western regiments of the King's Division: the King's Own Royal Border Regiment from Cumbria, the King's Regiment ('the Kingos') from Merseyside and Manchester, and the Queen's Lancashire Regiment. On initial establishment it had three regular battalions but in 2007 the third battalion was disbanded and its personnel distributed to the first and second battalions.

The KORBR and the QLR both had reputations as typically solid county regiments, with officers and soldiers predominantly recruited from their traditional recruiting areas. The Kingos, on the other hand, are somewhat more problematic: fine soldiers they undoubtedly are, but it's an undeniable fact that they had an Army-wide reputation for criminality that has survived the merger. Doubtless this is completely undeserved and simply represents deplorable anti-Scouse prejudice, but it has proved tenacious.

Scousers: the salt of the earth.

Beret: *khaki with regimental badge on a red diamond background.*
TRF: *KORBR glider.*

1 Lancs

Currently in the mechanized infantry role under 4 Mech Brigade based in Catterick.

2 Lancs

In the light infantry role based at Episkopi in the Western Sovereign Base Area in Cyprus.

RIFLE CLEANING

So, you've been issued a nice shiny L85A2 but it's not shiny enough, either because you fired it or because someone with stripes or crowns on their sleeve thinks it's a great idea to kill some time up to midnight. How do you do it?

According to the PAMs, of course! Lots of scrubbing with Scotchbrite and pullthroughs and rags, being careful not to use abrasives on any treated surfaces even though there is absolutely no other way of getting dirt off using what is provided. And lashings of light weapons oil, which has the cleaning properties of mud. In fact, in certain circumstances mud might even be better ...

But that method is balls and takes for ever!

The MoD has much better things to spend their money on than adequate rifle cleaning supplies, such as chairs. Or croquet sets. Or rifle components rendered unserviceable due to excess use of abrasives because they have no money for decent cleaning supplies. So it's scrubbing for you, sonny.

Perhaps I'm not asking the question correctly. So, let's say you were to own privately a nice shiny L85A2 that you have just befouled by taking it on a joyous range day in the blazing sunshine, with bucket loads of free ammunition. What would you personally do with it to bring it back to its former state of glory?

1 Strip the weapon down completely.

2 Place the gas plug and gas cylinder in a small container, add a wee dram of your favourite powder solvent (e.g. Brunox, Ballistol, 009, Hoppe's No. 9, Young's .303, BreakFree CLP, etc. NOT a metallic-fouling solvent like Sweet's or Robla Solo or anything else which smells strongly of ammonia. Mostly because they are unpleasant and possibly a little toxic, although myth frequently has it that they will dissolve your rifle on contact, which is nonsense otherwise people would not use them. Many powder solvents – like Brunox – claim that they will dissolve metallic fouling but their action is extremely mild and they are absolutely harmless to use on metallic parts, treated or not (again, if they were not, people would not use them). Give it a good shake to make sure everything is covered, and set it aside. These parts are the most heavily skanked up and will be dealt with last after the solvent has done the majority of the work for you.

3 If the chamber requires cleaning, use the chamber brush with some solvent on it. Then, using a Boresnake (a sort of uber-pullthrough), clean the barrel. Do this by putting some solvent on the start of the woven portion and pulling through several times. Even better – if your solvent comes in a squirty can you can squirt some of this down the barrel, leave it to soak a while, and then pull through. Do not attempt to put any cloth or anything else in the loop of the boresnake, because then it won't fit down the barrel in the case of 5.56mm and you will have what is commonly known as 'a serious problem'. The bore should now be nice and shiny. If it's not, either your Boresnake is filthy and requires cleaning (they're actually machine washable if you put them in a laundry bag), or you probably need to clean more. To do this you require a cleaning rod and a phosphor bronze brush in good condition and of the correct calibre. Normal pullthroughs are crap, which is why you won't see civilians use them. Soak the brush in solvent, push it all the way through the barrel and pull it all the way back about half a dozen times. Do not change the direction of the brush when it is in the bore, since this will knacker the brush. Contrary to popular belief, a phosphor bronze brush will not scratch the bore steel, unless the brush is full of grit and sand (in which case it's the grit and sand which are damaging the steel). Now, using a jag, and patches no larger than 40x40mm, dry the solvent out of the barrel. The vast majority of the crud will come with it, and the bore will look very shiny. Cruddy, damaged, worn, or old brushes should be replaced.

4 Using some rags with a dab of solvent on, clean the inside of the receiver, the bolt, the bolt carrier, the barrel extension, the spring guide rods, the outside of the barrel near the gas parts, the inside of the handguard near the gas parts, the TMH, and anything I have forgotten. You will be amazed at how easily the crud comes off. Useful things to have at hand for the awkward parts are your mate's toothbrush, cotton buds and pipe cleaners (which can be bent double and used to get into difficult places, such as under the extractor).

5 Give the gas vent hole a swizz with the reamer and a solvent-soaked cotton bud if you really insist – this part is inaccessible on most rifles, including the SLR, and never really causes a problem. The hole in the gas block into which the gas plug is engaged should also be cleaned as best you can with solvent.

6 Turning our attention now to the gas parts which have been busily stewing in solvent for the best part of 10 or 20 minutes, extract these from their container. The vast majority of the fouling should now wipe off, and you will find that a cotton bud fits rather nicely down the inside of the gas plug, where some of the nastiest fouling lurks. Using a rag and the combination tool, you should be able to get most of the crap out of the gas cylinder as well. Use the reamers on the combination tool to get at any baked on. The outside of the gas cylinder on the A2 is coated in black stuff (Teflon, apparently), so keep that dirty Scotchbrite away from it – the surface treatment is there for a reason and should remain there for the same reason.

7 Admire your shiny handiwork, oil up, including a thin film on the inside of the barrel, ensuring that all untreated steel parts have a thin layer of oil, and reassemble. Use the issue oil for this – it might have the cleaning properties of an encrusted wank sock, but it's actually a very good lubricant.

TRAINING

So you've made it through the recruiting process and ADSC – well done. But that was the easy bit. What comes next is going to be somewhat tougher.

Whatever trade you're going for and whatever qualifications and skills you bring with you, you aren't much use to the Army until you can function as a soldier with a shared set of basic skills. You acquire these through training.

Initial training falls into two broad parts. Phase 1 training consists of the basic common military skills required by all recruits, whether soldiers or officers (with the exception of professionally qualified officers – doctors, dentists, lawyers, vets and

Training: you can run but you can't hide.

so on) and is undertaken at one of the four Army Training Regiments (Bassingbourn, Lichfield, Pirbright, Winchester), the Army Foundation College at Harrogate, or, for officers, at Sandhurst; the exceptions to this are adult infantry recruits who do all of their training at the Infantry Training Centre Catterick. Phase 2 training is the specialist and technical training which trains soldiers for their chosen trade. This is sponsored by the individual regiments and corps and takes place within their own schools and training centres.

PHASE I

Phase 1 training for adult soldiers is a fourteen-week 'Common Military Syllabus' (CMS(R)) course during which they are taught the following basic skills:

- » Weapon handling and Application of Fire using the SA80A2 rifle

- » Physical fitness

- » Chemical, Biological, Radiological and Nuclear defence

- » Fieldcraft – the basics of living in the field

- » Battlefield Casualty Drills – basic first aid

- » Navigation and map reading

- » Foot drill

Adult recruits for the Royal Armoured Corps, Household Cavalry, REME and Royal Engineers go to ATR Bassingbourn in Cambridgeshire (this was where the training scenes for the Kubrick movie *Full Metal Jacket* were filmed). Adult recruits for the Royal Artillery, Royal Signals, RLC, Army Air Corps, Adjutant General's Corps, Intelligence Corps, Army Medical Services and Corps of Army Music do their Phase 1 training at Pirbright in Surrey, which used to be the Guards depot. Junior soldiers from all regiments and corps (including the infantry) either do a special twenty-three-week version of the CMS(R) course at ATR Winchester in Hampshire, or a forty-three-week course at the Army Foundation College, Harrogate, which includes additional education and leadership development modules.

I 100 per cent guarantee that the old sweats will tell you that training was much tougher in their day. Is this true? Nope: training standards have pretty much remained the same for the last twenty years, and in some ways have arguably got harder. What has changed is the way it's all presented. Twenty or thirty years ago basic training came across pretty much as a ferocious beasting, with the recruits being buggered around from pillar to post at all hours of the day and night by training NCOs and officers who largely seemed to have been close associates of the Marquis de Sade. This worked, in its way, but it also led to problems. Beasting easily became bullying and harassment, and these attitudes within the training establishments fed into the field army. It was never true that the Army was a hotbed of bullying, but it was there as a strong undercurrent.

What has changed, then, is that there is now a recognition that supporting recruits through the training process is just as successful as beasting them through it. This doesn't mean that nobody is going to shout at you if you fuck up – they will – but it does mean that nobody is going to take you round the back of the accommodation and kick the shit out of you for having a finger mark on your belt buckle, or anything stupid like that. Does this work? The proof is in the pudding: the old sweats who whinge about how 'easy' recruit training has become weren't being asked to put their lives on the line in high-intensity counter-insurgency operations as soon as they were out of training. There are no complaints about the quality of British soldiers in Afghanistan, and that's where it matters.

[LIVING THE ARMY LIFE]

INTERVIEW WITHOUT COFFEE

When everything is going swimmingly and your brigade commander/CO/Chief of Staff/RSM invites you to his (or her) office for a quick chat, chances are that you will be offered a 'brew'. Nothing fancy, normally; Nescafé Gold Blend in a mug would be about average. When things are really motoring, there's even the chance of a chocolate bourbon, custard cream or HobNob. Savour these moments!

A tell-tale sign that things aren't going so well is when no coffee is offered. Maybe you've just accidentally spunked the battalion's entire annual travel budget on the LAD day-trip to Skegness; perhaps your bright idea of getting some strippers to perform at the CO's leaving do has just got him on to the front page of the *News of the World*; possibly you've got the lowest grade ever on ICSC. Whatever the case, if there's no coffee, you're in the shit.

Of course, in these modern HR-driven times, when people are recognized as the Army's single greatest asset, it isn't going to be that bad, is it? Maybe not. Sometimes you may get away with an uncomfortable five minutes of tight-lipped invective to which the proper answer is either 'Yes, sir' or 'No, sir'. But don't be too sure. The true master of the 'interview without coffee' will leave his victim a quivering, weeping wreck. Instances of miscreants wetting themselves and even fainting are not unheard of.

Bang, bang! You're dead!

PHASE 2

The length and location of phase 2 training is defined by which trade a soldier is following. Thus, for example, Royal Artillery recruits go to Larkhill, Royal Signals personnel go to Blandford, Intelligence Corps recruits go to Chicksands, and so on. It's worth noting that recruits in both the Intelligence Corps and Royal Military Police are given immediate promotion to Lance Corporal on successful completion of their phase 2 training, reflecting the particular responsibilities of their trades.

The Combat Infantry Course

As noted earlier, recruits to the infantry complete their phase 1 and phase 2 training at the Infantry Training Centre Catterick, where they undertake the twenty-six-week Combat Infantryman's Course. This covers the basic Common Military Syllabus subjects and includes additional training in skill at arms, including support weapons, tactics, physical fitness and drill. Recruits for the Foot Guards do an additional two weeks of drill to reflect the ceremonial duties of the Household Division, while potential Parachute Regiment soldiers must pass the two-week 'Pre-Parachute Selection' course – aka P Company – which qualifies them to do the Basic Parachute Course.

[LIVING THE ARMY LIFE] HORROR BAG

An innocent-looking brown paper bag, or even a white cardboard box, looking rather like the sort of thing you might get cream cakes in from a craft baker. Instead they contain the usual items of an Army packed lunch:

- One cheap drink. Panda Cola, a drink that looks and smells a bit like real Coke but tastes like gaseous, sugared vultures' urine, is a favourite, but only in the sense that it's often used. Allegedly, 47p is allocated as an allowance for this item. Where the other 42p goes is one of the mysteries of military accounting.
- One pasty. Once upon a time these were made by Ginsters, but now tend to be cheap copies. Unlikely ever to have been within 200 miles of Cornwall; highly likely still to be frozen in the middle.
- One sandwich. Normal filling is mystery fish (see page 207); occasionally egg mayonnaise, cheese,

or value processed-ham-substitute.
- One KitKat/Blue Riband/Breakaway. Used solely to fool the unsuspecting recipient into thinking the other items are edible.
- One bag of crisps. Almost always salt and vinegar or cheese and onion. Always an unknown brand.
- A three-pack of slightly soft bourbons or custard creams.

Localized variants exist. In the north, the pasty is replaced by a sausage roll with pastry so flaky that as yet no way has been found to eat it without covering yourself in lethal shards of pâte brisée. This, too, will still be frozen in the middle. 'Meat' pasties and sausage rolls are allegedly required to contain no more than 10 per cent meat. Only meat recovered from ears, trotters, hooves and sphincters is used. The Sandhurst variant on this is something the young officer cadet will have nightmares about for the rest of his or her life.

THE YORKSHIRE REGIMENT

The Yorkshire Regiment was formed in 2006 from the remaining three regiments in the King's Division: the Prince of Wales's Own Regiment of Yorkshire, the Green Howards and the Duke of Wellington's Regiment. Again, like their north-western counterparts in the Lancs, these were three very traditional English county regiments with strong links to their recruiting areas. 'Appen the PWO and Duke of Boots thought that the Green Howards could be a bit la-di-dah (there was a strong rumour in the 1980s that Green Howards officers had been heard to suggest the regiment were 'the Yorkshire

Guards' but this was never satisfactorily proved). Unlike the Lancs, the Yorkshire Regiment managed to retain three regular battalions and thus maintain separate regimental identities, albeit with a shared cap-badge.

Beret: khaki with regimental badge on a green backing.

1 Yorks

Formerly 1 PWO and recruited from the triangle of Leeds, York and Hull, 1 Yorks are light role infantry based in Münster, Germany as part of 20 Armoured Brigade. 1 Yorks have traditionally been a good athletics battalion; at one stage, the British Olympian Kris Akabusi was attached to the battalion from the Army Physical Training Corps as QMSI.

The Officers' Mess of 1 Yorks has over the years developed a reputation as a somewhat ferocious place where young officers can have a torrid time. It would be idle to deny this but the battalion has nonetheless produced more than its share of fighting commanders, all of whom started out as hated 'red-arses' in the beginning.

Typical 1 Yorks black-tie night.

Chimpanzee or French spy? You decide.

2 Yorks

The Frankies; the Dingles; the Monkeyhangers

At the time of the 2006 merger, the Green Howards were one of only five line infantry battalions which had never previously been merged. The battalion primarily recruits in North Yorkshire up to the River Tees and is currently based in Weeton just outside Blackpool, as a light role infantry battalion with 11 Infantry Brigade. In recent years, the Green Howards managed to finesse a series of officers into top jobs in defence: Field Marshal Inge, the Chief of Defence Staff; General Dannatt, Chief of the General Staff; and General Houghton, Vice Chief of Defence Staff were all Frankies, creating a tradition not unlike the 'Black Mafia' of the Light Division.

3 Yorks

The Dukes; the Duke of Boots

The Dukes are currently based at Warminster as the armoured infantry battalion with 12 Mech Brigade. Traditionally, although recruiting from South Yorkshire and the West Riding – rugby league country – they have been one of the strongest rugby union battalions in the British Army.

4 Yorks

4 Yorks is the TA battalion recruited from across the regimental area. It was created from various TA infantry sub-units which over the last twenty years or so had been through a series of convulsive changes as the result of changing policies at the MoD. These have included being separate regiments in their own right at different periods (as, for example, the Yorkshire Volunteers or the West Riding Regiment) and being affiliated to the Yorkshire Regiment at others (for example, for a short period, one of the Yorkshire TA battalions became '3 PWO'). With yet another Defence Review imminent, who can guess how long the current situation will hold?

THE PRINCESS OF WALES'S ROYAL REGIMENT

The Tigers (what they call themselves); the Squidgies (what everyone else calls them)

The PWRR are the elegant offspring of the marriage of the Queen's Regiment (recruited in London and the Home Counties) and the Royal Hampshire Regiment (guess where they were recruited) in 1992. The two regular battalions of the PWRR are now the county regiment of Surrey, Kent, Middlesex, Hampshire, Sussex, the Isle of Wight and the Channel Islands.

The PWRR shot to fame when the gorgeous, pouting Princess Diana became their Colonel in Chief on their formation in 1992 and this spawned their unofficial nickname, 'the Squidgies' (after what a certain blackguard ex-Household Cav officer called her in the throes of passion). Diana retired from the military scene after her divorce, and although her successor as Mrs Prince Charles isn't the Princess of Wales, there's a strong momentum to rename the PWRR 'Camilla's Gorillas'.

Another claim to fame is 1 PWRR's operational tour in Maysan province, Iraq in 2004 during which Johnson Beharry, a private soldier in the battalion, won the VC and, so the rumour goes, every single member of the battlegroup was forced to fire their weapon in anger at one time or another. A solid, professional bunch with just a hint of the 'cockernee wide boy' among the officers and soldiers.

Beret: *khaki with regimental badge on a blue and yellow flash.*

LCpl Johnson Beharry VC (*left*): very, very brave.

1 PWRR

1 PWRR are based at Paderborn, Germany as an armoured infantry battalion with 20 Armoured Brigade.

2 PWRR

2 PWRR will, in the medium term, be rotating between a UK-based light infantry and public duties role, and the light role in Cyprus (handy for ravers, fun lovers and thrill seekers in the flesh-pots of Ayia Napa, Limassol, Paphos, etc.) garrisoning the Sovereign Base Areas and acting as a theatre reserve for the Middle East.

3 PWRR

A TA battalion covering the south-east corner of England, with the exception of London (one of the companies of the London Regiment is 'badged' as PWRR). Their headquarters is in Canterbury.

THE ROYAL REGIMENT OF FUSILIERS

The Budgies

The Royal Regiment of Fusiliers is one of the older regiments of the British Army, having been around since as long ago as 1968. You can spot Fusiliers a mile off because of the red and white hackle they wear in their berets – a fact

A Fusilier in a fit of indecision.

[LIVING THE ARMY LIFE] BIKINI STATE

Enter any military establishment and you will almost always see a board on display in or near the guardroom and/or reception desk headed 'Bikini State'. Strange as it may seem, this does not relate to the degree of body hair waxing mandated by the current Secretary of State, or mean that a beach volleyball tournament may be about to take place; it refers to the perceived level of terrorist threat to defence establishments.

The various states of alert are as follows:

- RED: imminent risk of attack
- AMBER: high threat of attack
- BLACK SPECIAL: average threat
- BLACK: minimum threat
- WHITE: no known threat

Each state carries with it a different level of security preparation, from white, which would effectively mean no extra security requirement, to red, at which point the inhabitants of a base start building a rampart of mealie bags and sharpening their bayonets.

---

not lost on enemy snipers, and a good reason for not wearing the hackle in combat. The RRF are the county regiment for London, central Lancashire, Warwickshire (including Birmingham) and Northumberland, which means that down to section level you'll hear a joyful cacophony of cockney, Manc, Brummie and Geordie accents. How wonderful!

Beret: dark blue with red and white hackle above regimental badge.

1 RRF

The first battalion is currently in the armoured infantry role and based in delightful Tidworth.

2 RRF

A light infantry battalion currently based at Cavalry Barracks, Hounslow, west London – one of the worst barracks in the British Army: rat-infested, falling down, and close enough to Heathrow Airport that the planes rattle your teeth when they fly over – in a public-duties role. Their role will see them periodically rotate out to Cyprus to join the garrison there.

5 RRF

5 RRF is the TA battalion of the regiment formed from the 'Tyne-Tees Regiment' which enjoyed a fairly brief existence in the early 2000s. Although formally RRF, it is a multi-cap-badged regiment.

YOU'RE IN THE ARMY NOW

THE KIT

Allyness

Allyness ('ally' is pronounced to rhyme with 'Sally') is best described as military fashion sense, i.e. wearing various non-issue items, or modifying issue clothing or equipment, in order to look subtly different from one's peers. This can cause chaos when the entire battalion is trying to do the same thing: 'Oh my God! He's wearing the same smock as me!'

Many, if not all, champions of allyness will argue that they aren't doing it for the look, but rather because the standard-issue items are either not up to the job or aren't as good as the kit that they've bought. Some, especially those of a more Walty cast of mind, are keen to subtly suggest that they wear ally gear because it was issued to them when they were doing some special super secret task.

Sometimes issue items can become ally simply by being used in a theatre other than where they are usually issued, for example the wearing of jungle combats or Falklands parkas in the UK. On the other hand, wearing jungle combats

Ally as fuck!

in the Falklands, or a Falklands parka in the jungle, would not be in the least ally.

You see, there's a fine line between ally and stupid, i.e. between looking the business (even if you don't have a clue what you're doing) and looking like a big-timing Walty twat. There was a time when it almost became acceptable within certain circles to put chains in the bottoms of one's OG trousers to ensure that they hung straight. It looked odd, and sounded even odder, with blokes chinking and clanking around camp with weighted lightweights – which is sort of oxymoronic. This was decidedly non-ally behaviour, verging on silliness.

Typical ally items include:

》 SAS smocks – the perennial favourite. Has anyone actually ever used the hood?

》 Para smocks, especially if you're not a Para, and obviously the bigger the better. In reality, Para smocks are no better than standard combat jackets in any meaningful way.

》 Arctic windproofs. Very much in vogue after the Falklands War.

》 Tropical combats, tailored and bleached to pastel shades.

》 DPM Flying jackets.

》 Flying boots.

》 Jungle boots.

》 Jungle hats with the brim and crown cut down.

》 Woolly beanie hats.

》 Pace beads.

》 Beta lights.

》 Assault vests – although now that they're widely issued their allyness score has dropped markedly.

》 Machetes and/or big combat knives, especially Gurkha kukris, although these can look ridiculous.

》 Thigh holsters.

》 Shemaghs.

》 Officers' berets.

》 Para helmets.

》 DILAC hats – yes, there was a renaissance.

》 Hi-Tec Trail boots.

》 Mega sideys, huge gaucho 'taches, and tour beards.

Champions of allyness include (but are not limited to) the SAS, the SBS, the Parachute Regiment and the Royal Marines.

Back in the day, soldiers wanted to be mistaken for Special Forces because they were the only dudes likely to get serious combat, and the whole point of being ally was looking like an experienced veteran, but with Iraq and now Afghanistan, more

PLCE rucksack: surprisingly good.

Norway and issued to commando, airborne and SAS units and formations involved in arctic and mountain warfare. These people got an issue rucksack because they were much better for load carrying than the issue '37, '44 and '58 Pattern large packs. No sensible person has yet been able to explain what the advantages of 'large packs' for other formations were.

In the 1970s, the rucksack GS and the rucksack SAS began to be issued as above, but also to units conducting rural patrols in Northern Ireland. These rucksacks featured a butyl nylon sack mounted on an external GS manpack frame which was also used for Clansman radios and ECM equipment. The GS rucksack had a capacity of about 60 litres while the SAS rucksack could hold about 120 litres. They carried the weight high on the back above the '58 Pattern kidney pouches.

After the Falklands War, where transport problems forced most soldiers to carry all of their equipment, most of the time, the Army began to get sensible about rucksacks. A large number of Berghaus and Karrimor rucksacks were purchased 'off-the-shelf' while a new infantry rucksack was designed, ~~stolen from~~ based on the commercial Crusader design. This was followed a few years later by the smaller 'other arms' rucksack, aka the REMF's Handbag.

A significant problem with big bergens is that soldiers stuff them

rounds have been going down the two-way range in a couple of weeks than were fired in the entire thirty years of the Northern Ireland campaign and there's a bit of ally in everyone who's done an operational tour now.

What does the future hold? The classic DPM, which has basically served the British Army well for half a century, is in the process of being superseded by 'Multi-Terrain Pattern' (MTP), a camouflage designed to work well in temperate, tropical and desert environments. Call me Nostradamus, but I guess that in ten years' time ally officers and NCOs will be wearing old DPM gear . . .

The Bergen

The original bergens were A-frame rucksacks made by Bergen of

with all kinds of unnecessary clutter which they never actually use, and the trend now is towards intermediate-sized rucksacks, like the superb Infantry Patrol Pack which is now on limited issue.

Boots, Boots, Boots, Boots, Marchin' Up and Down Again . . .

Back in the early half of the twentieth century, a soldier would be issued with two pairs of leather-soled hobnailed ammo boots. One pair would be double-soled and bulled to a perfect mirror-shine as his best boots, the other pair would be greased and waterproofed for use in the field. The boots were ankle height and reasonably well made out of good leather, but of course were too low to offer much waterproofing and thus were generally supplemented by gaiters, anklets or puttees.

At some point in the late 1950s or early 1960s some genius within either the Army or MoD decided that our boots needed updating, but instead of going for a modern high-leg design with sewn-in tongue, which offers great waterproofing and protection advantages and was in use in just about every other army in the world from Andorra to Zambia, decided to keep the basic shape of the antiquated ammo boots but fit them with a rubber 'Direct Moulded Sole'. Oh yes, and they made them out of lower-quality leather as well. Thus were born Boots DMS (also alleged to mean 'Dem's Ma Shoes'). The suggestion that anyone thought that Boots DMS were a good idea is beyond belief. For a start it meant that in a modern, late-twentieth-century army every soldier had to spend a couple of minutes every morning wrapping a brown wool puttee around each ankle. Much more seriously, however, during the Falklands Conflict in 1982 trench foot reared its ugly head again after a sixty-five-year absence, because troops were unable to keep their feet dry for weeks on end as the result of wearing crappy, non-waterproofable ankle boots.

In fact by then a replacement was already in the pipeline, and in 1984 issue began of the Boot Combat High, or 'BCH'. The first of these were pretty good, sturdily made of strong leather, but they did have several drawbacks. For a start, the design was such that for some soldiers, creases in the rear of the boot put a great deal of pressure on the Achilles tendon, leading to acute

Issued combat boots: really shit.

tendonitis and other lower-leg injuries, particularly when they were used for running; they were also difficult to break in and could give severe blisters to the unwary.

Combat Soldier 95: so good even senior officers wear it.

Several minor redesigns followed, and soldiers – particularly recruits – were generally discouraged from doing any kind of PT while wearing boots. However, simultaneously, as manufacturers sought to maximize profits and MoD tried to cut costs, quality of manufacture dropped to the extent that nowadays, whenever the British Army goes on a major operation, they buy in suitable commercially made footwear from makers like Lowa and Danner. The current-issue boots are so poorly made that their rubber soles have a very limited lifespan and after a while disintegrate and fall off. Impressive, huh? Anyone buying their own boots now would do well to look at those made by Lowa, Meindl, Alt-berg and Danner, and, for the more budget-conscious, Magnum. If properly fitted, these are likely to be somewhat more comfortable than the issue efforts, and distinctly harder wearing.

Combat Soldier 95

Before you slag it off, would you like to go back to lightweights, 'Hairy Maries' (woolly shirts), shrink-easy jumpers and crisp-packet (non-breathable polyurethane) water-proofs? Thought not.

The Combat 95 clothing system has to satisfy stringent military requirements covering infra-red reflection (IRR), thermal signature and flame resistance. It is based on the layer principle and is designed to provide the soldier with exactly the right degree of protection for any operational environment. This had previously been only half-heartedly considered with such awesome kit as the Chinese fighting jacket and trousers (a quilted suit that was worn underneath the combat suit), but without much success.

Combat 95 was something of a revolution in the British Army, in that it is supposedly almost 'bullshit' free. It's practical, comfortable and good. As a result it has almost completely replaced any other form of dress in most units. Most soldiers' ideal field kit before this was tropical trousers, green fleeces and windproof smocks, and CS95 provides a very close match for that, but it's issued to everyone and you don't have to shell out for it. Excellent, although a little late, and the jacket has an unfeasibly large neck hole.

Combat 95 consists of the following items:

» A high-tech 'wicking' T-shirt (soldiers, male and female, are expected to provide their own shreddies – shame: I wonder what an issue DPM thong would look like?).

» Comfy socks.

» A 'Norgie' shirt (loop-stitched cotton shirt with a zip-up roll-neck collar).

» A DPM lightweight shirt/jacket based on the tropical combat shirt but with a rank slide on the front rather than the shoulders.

» A pair of DPM trousers.

» A green or DPM fleece jacket.

» A DPM combat jacket in 'rip-stop' material (and now with a hood, much like the issue SAS smock). No lie, this is the kind of kit we would have killed for when I first joined the Army!

» A nice pair of Gore-tex lined leather gloves.

» A set of DPM waterproof jacket and trousers in 'vapour-permeable material' (i.e. Gore-tex, or something amazingly similar). We'd have killed for this, too!

» A pair of really shit boots.

Inevitably, having come up with an innovative and practical approach to the long-vexed issue of clothing us in a workable way, the Army then let loose the dogs of tradition. The lightweight jacket has effectively become a shirt, worn tucked in – even in the field – and often with a garish stable belt. Inevitably, RSMs like to see CS95 clobber ironed to within an inch of its existence, which wears it out at an exponential rate, and there is a distressing tendency for it to sprout badges, the effect of which is to make squaddies look like militant cub scouts.

Some of this may be mitigated by the Army's oft-voiced intention of acquiring a cheap-but-smart form of dress to be worn as barrack dress (basically the green shirts and lightweight trousers we used to wear during the seventies, eighties and early nineties), leaving CS95 to be worn in the field as it was meant to be, but with the financial situation being what it is at present, don't hold your breath.

Dangerous Brian Hat: say no more.

Dangerous Brian Hat

Very large camouflage headwear with long earflaps which can be Velcroed over the top of the head, making the wearer look a bit like a paramilitary lumberjack – and, of course, utterly ridiculous.

While undeniably warm, DB hats are lined with the world's most itchy substance (developed at Porton Down to be smuggled into Soviet military underwear factories, thus adding an interesting paragraph to the Russian equivalent of the chemical safety rule).

Dangerous Brian hats were of course banned by many COs on the grounds of sheer stupidity, but continue to be the perfect comple-ment to a Chinese fighting jacket and issue long-johns while drink-ing a Red Bull and vodka in the Officers' Mess. They are regularly used to accessorize a 'Naked Bar', particularly in RM messes.

Also known as the Deputy Dawg Hat (or Dawg Hat for short).

GS Blankets

Using a GS blanket is like trying to sleep inside a bath of hungry ants. Originally knitted during the Boer War out of barbed wire, these sons of bitches are indestructible and have been around ever since. Why do you think quilts are banned on training courses? It gives the cadre something to chuckle over, especially when they see your skin rash on PT. They can be used to wax and shine a floor, remove rust from metal, put out kitchen fires, as a barrier against nerve gas and to isolate molten lava, but not for sleeping in. Many claim that examples of Roman Army standard-issue GS blankets have been dug up by members of Channel 4's *Time Team*, reclaimed by the Ministry of Defence and issued to Army training establishments around the country.

Hexamine

Top stuff. Don't be fooled. Buggering around with Gucci petrol stoves is simply not worth it unless you are some kind of mountain warrior. Hexy is short for hexamine, a kind of solid fuel which allegedly (according to the powers that be) burns cleanly and leaves no residue or ash. It certainly burns, releasing copious amounts of noxious fumes, and while it's true there is no ash or residue left on the ground, this is because the residue has migrated to your mess

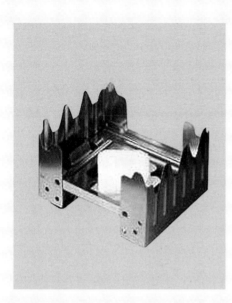

was decided during the Malayan Emergency to introduce a special boot designed for such an environment. The result was a curious bright-green canvas-and-rubber affair that looked similar to baseball boots but with a very high leg. They were not very successful, but they did have their plaudits and they were better than sloshing around the bondu in ammo boots or Boots DMS.

Hexy cooker: great when you need to make your mess tins dirty.

These boots lingered on until the superior US-manufactured classic Vietnam jungle boot became widely available. I first encountered this incarnation in the early eighties, when the bemused onlooker was astounded by a US Marine sporting a pair of the most ally-looking daps he'd ever seen. He simply just had to have a pair of those. Said Marine was not willing to part with his footwear,

tin, which is now coated in thick immovable black goo.

Hexy telly – staring into the flames to while away the long night hours on exercise – is the recreational use of hexamine. Many claim to be able to read the future while in a hexy telly-induced trance (quite often the future seems to consist of a mess tin coated in thick black goo and a lukewarm cup of tea, but you can't have everything). The perfect accompaniment to an evening in front of the hexy telly is of course gruff nut removal and sucking boilies until your gums bleed.

Jungle Boots

Environment-specific footwear didn't really make an appearance until the 1960s; prior to this the general-issue boot had to make do in all terrains and weathers. Jungles being nasty, wet, horrible places, it

Jungle boots: well ally.

but it wasn't long before I managed to get my hands on a pair. They certainly turned heads in the mess, especially when worn in January with a set of tropical trousers and a parka! Top that! The boots really came into their own during a Belize tour. Sashaying around Airport Camp while sporting the epitome of tropical pedal attire was certainly a better option than the DMS alternative.

During a visit by Phil the Greek, the Guard of Honour were issued with the elusive and mythical jungle boots, albeit the green US-made variety. They were duly ordered to polish the canvas to black, thus ruining the rot-proofing and totally fucking up perfectly serviceable (and brand-new) boots. After the parade they were made to hand them back in and they were never seen again. Simply scaling everyone with jungle boots being far too obvious an option, the hapless wearers reverted to their less than sartorially elegant DMS footwear.

Not so me. By having privately purchased my 'genuine' junglies (from Silverman's) I'd avoided such humiliation and by the end of the tour they'd been lovingly scrubbed so much that the canvas sides were almost faded to white. Well ally.

The affair could not last, however, and they fell to pieces. Efforts to exchange them were fruitless, and they were last seen being sported by a Boon in the Big Apple.

Being British, of course, we decided to make our own version of the US jungle boot and came out with something that appeared to be a DMS boot with the ankle bit removed and replaced with green canvas, which made it look like a slightly more ally NHS orthopaedic shoe. Under rigorous jungle conditions these lasted about 14.7 seconds so combat arms personnel posted to Belize were finally, and very grudgingly, issued with US jungle boots, which they actually got to keep. Woo hoo!

Nowadays the jungle boot has been modernized by the substitution of black cordura for the old green canvas, but they still exude an air of ally 'been-thereness' when sported as part of a staff officer's working dress ensemble, particularly if the soles have been worn away to virtually nothing.

No. 2 Dress

Aaaahhhh, the much-fabled 'Ginger Marching Suit', beloved of generations of chafed squaddies.

The Army's basic smart uniform, No. 2 Dress (so-called because it's the same colour as baby shit) is loosely modelled on a cross between the pre-WW2 officers and ORs Service Dress, which was actually a field uniform. No. 2 Dress consists of a khaki tunic and trousers, worn with a khaki shirt and tie, regimental head-dress and highly polished boots (or shoes if you're an officer). Most regiments and corps have nice shiny buttons (which don't have to be polished) as well as regimental collar badges (often called 'collar dogs') which are occasionally completely

[LIVING THE ARMY LIFE] IRANIAN MARS BARS

Originally produced as part of a contract for the Shah of Iran in the late 1970s, these Mars bars were never delivered and instead made their way into compo twenty-four-hour packs where they could be found well into the mid-1990s, by which time they had developed an outer layer of fine white powder and tasted like mothballs. A Royal Marine chappie I used to work with fed one of these to Buster, my black Labrador, causing him to fart so violently we were forced to evacuate the office temporarily.

different to their cap-badges. Scottish regiments, of course, wear a tartan kilt or trews; a few other regiments wear odd-coloured trousers.

The ginger marching suit.

Officers and WO1s generally wear either a Sam Browne or crossbelt in No. 2 Dress, while other ranks are normally to be seen in a green or white waist belt, often with a regimental buckle.

Until recently, officers bought their 'Service Dress' from private tailors, and were given a BFO grant to do so. The plan now is that officers and ORs will be issued the same 'Service Dress', which will presumably save a few quid for the Defence budget but put a few more tailors on the dole for the Social Security budget. Decisions, decisions!

Sleeping System

Aka 'the Green Maggot' or 'the Bouncing Bomb', the sleeping system consists of a big, green, artificially filled sleeping bag with a compression sack, a Gore-tex bivvy bag, a sleeping mat and a poncho. All very roasty-toasty. Once a soldier is in one of these it can be hard to extract him. Interestingly enough, after a year or two the average Army sleeping bag contains enough of a soldier's DNA to construct an exact 1/6th-scale replica, just like Mini Me.

It is not uncommon for the toe-end of the bag to contain a well-used wank sock (see opposite).

Tropical Combats

Some time in the 1970s the British Army decided to update its tropical combat uniform from the old green cotton denim suit to a somewhat more modern, DPM-camouflaged number. Thus were born tropical combats which for an extended period from the early 1980s onwards

Tropical combats: prehistoric ally.

were officially the British Army's ally-est rig.

They consisted of nothing more than a lightweight shirt/jacket, a pair of baggy trousers with a map pocket on both legs, and a camouflaged bush hat. All very simple. The great thing about them, as experience soon showed, was that through repeated washing, the camouflage print became a bright, garish, almost fluorescent colour while the clothes themselves became soft and slightly shapeless.

What was ally about this? Well, it either meant that you'd done an exotic-ish tour in Belize or Brunei, or that you were in the SAS, who were the only people who regularly trained in the jungle apart from those in Belize or Brunei – or maybe even both. Result! And a highly visible result too! They were also much better made than the temperate combat kit which was issued from the mid-eighties to the mid-nineties, which was, not to put too fine a point on it, utterly shite.

Of course, it wasn't all win-win. The bravura coloration of tropical combats made them the bane of every RSM's existence and a low-level insurgency was fought out between the lads, whose natural instincts are generally towards the ally, and the middle management, who usually aim for uniformity. Junior officers would often side with the lads in this, but even then the situation could be delicately balanced.

The introduction of CS95 took some of the ally wind out of the sails of tropical combats – not least because the design was explicitly based on them – but even today you will see officers and NCOs *d'un certain âge* sporting their bright yellow and green 'trops' with pride.

And finally... L1A1 Green Sock Conversion

It can be boring and lonely on exercises and operations, and inevitably a soldier's mind will turn at such moments to thoughts of a carnal nature. But what to do with any bodily products that ensue? Step forward the wank sock. Converted from the standard-issue L1A1 Green Sock, the sacrificial sock has been thickly coated with nature's varnish to provide a relatively waterproof receptacle for the products of the British soldier's occasional forays into the recesses of his dark imagination. As well as lurking near the foot of the soldier's sleeping bag, wank socks are often to be found in the built-in wank-sock pockets so thoughtfully provided by Her Majesty's Government.

When the trusty old wank sock is nowhere to be found, other items have been known to take its place:

» Tinned Compo Sausages and Beans. Simply remove the sausage in the middle, and do the deed. Points to note include: watch your testicles on the tin's sharp edges. DIY castrations have a tendency to cause unimaginable pain. It also adds

to the pleasure if you can get the tin to the right temperature. If you do choose to heat the tin up prior to molesting it then be sure not to overdo it: genital scalding will be classified as a self-inflicted injury. Another point to note: if someone offers you an open tin of the said product then don't think they are being friendly with you, it will more than likely have a certain extra something in it that isn't stated in the ingredients list on the tin.

» Tesco Bags. Desperate times call for desperate measures... When you're out of tinned food and your socks look like they've been blasted with an industrial-sized tin of starch, you can always rely on your trusty polythene friend.

» Peperami Wrapper. For the less well-endowed members of HM Forces.

A wank sock awaiting conversion.

The Royal Anglican Regiment: an artist's impression.

THE ROYAL ANGLIAN REGIMENT
The Angle Irons

The Royal Anglians are the county regiment for Bedfordshire, Cambridgeshire, Essex, Hertfordshire, Leicestershire, Lincolnshire, Norfolk, Northamptonshire, Rutland and Suffolk. They were formed as long ago as 1964 as the first of the newly conceived 'large infantry regiments' and originally fielded four regular and three TA battalions. This has been reduced over the years and the regiment is now composed of two regular and one TA battalions.

Much offence is regularly given to the regiment – and much hilarity to the rest of the Army – by the seemingly unbreakable habit of politicians and the media of referring to them as the Royal 'Anglicans'. Somehow this always seems to undermine the feeling that an expression of regret when a soldier is killed, for example, is genuine.

Beret: *khaki with black backing to regimental badge.*

1 R Anglian

The first battalion, 'the Vikings', are currently based at Bulford, a military garrison on the edge of the Salisbury Plain in Wiltshire whose only claim to fame is that it isn't Tidworth. The Vikings are a mechanized infantry battalion subordinate to 12 Mech Brigade.

2 R Anglian

2 R Anglian are in the light role subordinate to 7 Armoured Brigade in Celle, near Hanover, Germany.

3 R Anglian

The TA element of the Royal Anglians has been through various permutations since there were three battalions of volunteers in the 1960s. After a brief period as the 'East of England Regiment' it is now back to being a single battalion, cap-badged Royal Anglian.

THE ROYAL WELSH

Anything to do with sheep-shagging; the Rarely Welsh (officers only)

We've all seen *Zulu* where a plucky handful of Welsh soldiers from the South Wales Borderers hold off thousands of Zulu warriors for a day and night while singing rugby songs in close harmony, winning against the odds when a larger force of Brits were being massacred nearby at Isandlhwana. Marvellous stuff! Except that only a handful of the soldiers at Rorke's Drift were Welsh: they were actually the second battalion of the Warwickshire Regiment and became the South Wales Borderers a couple of years later. Still, it's a good story.

Phwooar, jailbait!

The Royal Welsh are the modern iteration of the South Wales Borderers, amalgamated with the Welch Regiment (originally into the 'Royal Regiment of Wales') and more recently the Royal Welch Fusiliers. They were established as a new large infantry regiment on St David's Day, 2006, with two regular battalions and one TA.

To nobody's great surprise, the Royal Welsh are one of the great powerhouses of Army rugby. They also have a strange affinity with goats.

Beret: *khaki with regimental badge on a green backing.*

1 R Welsh

1 R Welsh are the old Royal Welch Fusiliers, currently in the light role with 11 Brigade and permanently based at Chester, conveniently close to their traditional recruiting area in North Wales (they recruit from the whole of Wales nowadays). Regular scrum downs with the Taliban form their current operational diet.

2 R Welsh

Formerly the Royal Regiment of Wales, 2 R Welsh are based at Lucknow Barracks, Tidworth as the armoured infantry battalion with 1 Mech Brigade.

3 R Welsh

The Welsh TA infantry battalion, with locations throughout Wales.

THE MERCIAN REGIMENT

The Mercians are effectively the geographical opposite of the Royal Anglian Regiment, being the result of the amalgamation in 2007 of the

A Mercian in his natural environment.

Cheshires, the Worcestershire and Sherwood Foresters ('the Woofers') and the Staffords, together with the 'West Midlands Regiment' of the TA. Although all three regular regiments came together under a single cap-badge, they were not downsized and have retained, to some extent, their individual identities. At the time of the amalgamation the Cheshires were the last remaining line infantry regiment that had never been amalgamated.

Beret: *khaki with regimental badge on Lincoln green backing.*

1 Mercian

Formerly the Cheshires, they are in the light role based at Catterick as part of 4 Mech Brigade.

2 Mercian

The Woofers are a light role infantry battalion assigned to 19 Light Brigade, based in Holywood Barracks on the outskirts of Belfast in Northern Ireland.

3 Mercian

The Staffords are based at Fallingbostel in northern Germany, near Hanover, as an armoured infantry battalion with the mighty 7 Armoured Brigade.

4 Mercian

The TA battalion of the Mercian Regiment is a multi cap-badge regiment, with E Company in Shrewsbury badged as 'Rifles' and A Company in Birmingham wearing the beret and hackle of the Royal Fusiliers.

THE ROYAL IRISH REGIMENT

The last of the Irish line infantry regiments, the Royal Irish were established in 1992 from the amalgamation of the Royal Irish Rangers and the Ulster Defence Regiment which had been created in the 1970s as a locally recruited volunteer force for operations in Northern Ireland. This created two regular battalions, two TA battalions and seven 'home service' battalions, although these were steadily reduced in number until 2007 when the final three 'resident battalions' (as the home service battalions had been renamed) were disbanded, leaving one regular and one TA battalion.

Traditionally the Royal Irish have recruited from among Northern Irish Protestants, but throughout the 'Troubles' there were always a substantial number of Catholics and citizens of the Irish Republic serving in the regular battalions and this has continued to the present day. (Catholics in the UDR were as rare as rocking-horse shit, on the other hand.)

Head-dress: a dark green 'caubeen' with a green hackle and regimental cap-badge. In the field they wear a more practical rifle green beret.

The caubeen: like a sack of spuds with a feather duster sticking out of it. Quintessentially Irish.

1 R Irish

The regular battalion of the Royal Irish are currently in the light role with 16 Air Assault Brigade and based at Tern Hill in north Shropshire, a barracks situated close to the throbbing metropolises of Shrewsbury, Telford and Market Drayton. And if that isn't exciting enough, it's not all that far from the Müller yogurt factory either.

2 R Irish

The TA battalion of the Royal Irish have their headquarters in Portadown and company locations across Northern Ireland.

THE PARACHUTE REGIMENT
The Paras; the Maroon Machine

Probably the most recognizable regiment in the British Army as a result of their maroon berets and winged parachute cap-badge, the Paras are very much a legend in their own lunchtime. The glamour of the Paras is widely resented throughout the British infantry, who point out, quite rightly, that other than parachuting (and the pre-parachute selection course, P Company) the Paras are trained in much the same way as every other infantry regiment. Unfortunately, this is only true up to a point. P Company is no stroll in the park: to get through it soldiers need to be highly motivated; and the glamour of the regiment is such that officer places are always oversubscribed, meaning that the Paras usually get to choose the pick of the litter from the Commissioning Course at Sandhurst.

This isn't to say that the Paras don't have their share of absolute cocks – they do – but their cock-quotient is probably lower than average. The Paras recruit from throughout the UK, and the Commonwealth too.

The second thing to say is that military parachuting is pretty much a thing of the past. It does have some limited utility for small-scale Special Forces operations, but we aren't going to see anything like Arnhem again. Today's Paras are primarily helicopter-borne air assault troops. The current tempo of operations and shortage of suitable aircraft means that the amount of parachute training available to the Army has been drastically reduced.

Beret: *maroon with regimental badge.*

1 Para

The 1st battalion of the Parachute Regiment was re-roled in 2006 as the core unit of the Special Forces Support Group. In effect, these are infantrymen selected and trained to provide infantry support to SAS, SBS and SRR operations. The intention is that members of 2 and 3 Para will be rotated through this role throughout their careers in order to ensure that the skills are passed to as wide a group as possible. 1 Para is based with the SFSG at St Athan in South Wales.

2 Para

The battalion that held the north end of the Arnhem Bridge and took Goose Green is currently in the air assault role and based in ritzy new accommodation in Colchester, Essex.

3 Para

'Gungy 3' are also in the air assault role and based in Colchester. 3 Para Mortar Platoon has for many years borne a reputation for the interesting entertainments favoured by its members. This is highly unfair: pretty much the same things go on throughout the battalion.

4 Para

The TA battalion of the Parachute Regiment has a well-established system providing individual reinforcements for the regular battalions when they deploy on operations. 4 Para has companies based in London, the north of England and Scotland. Like the regular battalions, a high degree of motivation is necessary rather than desirable to get through training.

THE ROYAL GURKHA RIFLES

Johnnie Gurkha

The RGR (and the Gurkha Signals, Engineers and Logistics units) are the last surviving element, in British service, of the old British Indian Army, which itself grew out of the East India Company Army. When India became independent of the UK in 1947 the Gurkha regiments of the Indian Army were divided between the British Army and the new Indian Army. The RGR was created as a two-battalion regiment in 1994 from the amalgamation of the four surviving Gurkha regiments.

A Gurkha with a big chopper.

Like the Paras, the Gurkhas have a unique glamour, but of course the only Brits who join them do so as officers: all the soldiers are Nepalese, and there are hundreds of applicants for each available place. Officers are a mixture of Brits and Gurkhas who either commission as DEs through Sandhurst or as LEs (the old system of QGOs has been abolished).

The stereotypical Gurkha soldier is smiling, cheerful, hard-working and polite. Well, yeah, but don't let this fool you: they are hard little fuckers who can get up to as much shit as anyone in the RHF or Kingos – be warned!

1 RGR

1 RGR are based in Brunei as the principal component of Britain's last garrison in South East Asia. Primarily trained for the jungle warfare role, they nevertheless have regularly deployed to Afghanistan as part of Op Herrick.

2 RGR

Based in Shorncliffe, near Folkestone, 2 RGR rotate between the light role and the air assault role in 16 Air Assault Brigade.

THE RIFLES

The Arfurs; the Black Mafia; the Rivets

The Rifles is the result of a seemingly endless series of amalgamations which has seen the old rifle regiments (the Light Infantry and the Royal Greenjackets) being folded in with the surviving descendants of various line infantry 'county' regiments from the west of England. The net result is that the Rifles are now the 'county' regiment for Cornwall, Devon, Dorset, Somerset, Gloucestershire, Herefordshire, Oxfordshire, Berkshire, Wiltshire, Shropshire, South Yorkshire, Durham and Buckinghamshire. Enough for you? The net result of all this is a seven-battalion (five regular, two TA) infantry regiment with a recruiting footprint spread around England like a madwoman's shite. The enormous footprint of the Rifles means that they also feature as Rifles cap-badged companies in 4 Mercian and 5 RRF as well as on about 30 per cent of Army Cadet Force detachments.

The Rifles: your local regiment if you live here.

Traditionally the rifle regiments recruited officers who were by reputation slightly less socially grand than Guards officers but somewhat cleverer, resulting in them being very successful at grabbing the top jobs in the Army (hence the nickname Black, or 'Black Button', Mafia). This is probably less true now than it once was.

Beret: *rifle green with regimental cap-badge. There are myriad regimental distinctions in various orders of dress from predecessor regiments.*

1 Rifles

Based at Chepstow in Monmouthshire, 1 Rifles is the bastard child of the amalgamation of the Devon and Dorset Light Infantry and the Royal Gloucester, Berkshire and Wiltshire Light Infantry (aka 'the M4 Rifles' or 'the Rivets' because of the 'back badge' of the Glosters), neither of which was a traditional rifle regiment.

1 Rifles has a unique role for an Army battalion as the fourth manoeuvre battalion within the Royal Marines 3 Commando Brigade. As a result, members of the battalion are put through the all-arms commando course and the battalion is being collectively trained in the Commando disciplines of arctic, mountain and amphibious warfare. Speculation that 1 Rifles would get jiffed for all the shitty jobs by their bootie comrades has been fiercely refuted. We'll see.

2 Rifles

2 Rifles, formerly 1 RGJ, are a light role battalion subordinated to 19 Light Brigade and based at Ballykinler in County Down, Northern Ireland, where the mountains of Mourne come down to the sea. Legend in the Army is that if you're in Ballykinler and you can't see the Mourne Mountains then it's raining, whereas if you can see them it's either just stopped raining or it's just about to start.

3 Rifles

3 Rifles are effectively the successor battalion to the old Durham and King's Own Yorkshire Light Infantry. They are based in Edinburgh as a light role battalion with 11 Light Brigade.

4 Rifles

4 Rifles are mechanized infantry based in Bulford, Wiltshire, the new name for 2 RGJ which recruits from London and the south-east (and thus seventy minutes' transit time from home up the A303/M3 on a Friday afternoon – vroooooom!). 4 Rifles are subordinated to 1 Mech Brigade.

5 Rifles

The former 1 LI are an armoured infantry battalion with 20 Armoured Brigade based in Paderborn. Recruited from Shropshire and the West Country, they are, like the old 3 RTR, nicknamed the 'Armoured Farmers'.

6 Rifles

6 Rifles are in effect the TA infantry battalion for the West Country, with elements in Gloucestershire, Wiltshire, Somerset, Dorset, Devon and Cornwall.

ANTI-TANK

84MM MAW SPECIFICATION	
Function:	Anti-tank weapon
Weight:	8.5 kg
Length overall:	1.1 m
Calibre:	84mm
Crew:	Two (gunner and loader), but may be used by a single operator at a reduced rate of fire.
Muzzle velocity:	230–255 m/s (750–840 ft/s)
Rate of fire rounds per minute:	6

84mm MAW

84mm recoilless Medium Anti-Tank Weapon, also known as the Carl Gustav, and in British service as the 'Charlie G'. Swedish-manufactured and used worldwide, the Carl Gustav was introduced in 1946 and was adopted by the Swedish Defence Force in 1948. The first prototypes used barrels from an old fort's cannons in Tingstäde, Gotland. The fort's four 8.4cm cannons (m/94-06) were used, hence the choice of calibre on the weapon – 84mm.

Largely obsolete and used by the British Army until the introduction of the LAW80 (see opposite).

Not a weapon to be dicked for carrying. Its finest hour was being used in the anti-shipping role by the Royal Marines during the Argentinian invasion of the Falkland Islands in 1982. It was also used in the Congo (1960–64), Indonesia, Afghanistan and Iraq.

ANTI-TANK

THE HARDWARE → [WEAPONS AND WEAPONS SYSTEMS]

LAW80 SPECIFICATION	
Calibre:	94mm
Firing mode:	1.5m
Launcher length:	1.5m firing 1m carrying
Carrying mode:	1m
Weight:	Carrying weight: 10kg Shoulder weight: 9kg Projectile weight: 4.6kg
Warhead arming range:	10–20m
Effective range:	20–500m
Fuze:	Type: Piezo-electric impact fuze, scrub- and foliage-proof
Graze angle:	<= 10°
Temperature range:	-46°C to +65°C
Rear danger area:	< 20m
Shelf life:	10 years

LAW80

The LAW80 is a 'one-shot' anti-tank weapon introduced to replace the Carl Gustav. It's clever in that it incorporates a spotting rifle, ballistically matched to the rocket, which is used to take 'sighter' shots at the target before the rocket is used. The warhead can supposedly penetrate up to 700mm (i.e. more than two feet) of armour plate. It would be idle to deny that this is a heavy and unwieldy beast but it does pack a substantial punch against armour and static positions.

Milan

Wire-guided AT missile. That's right, a long wire comes out the back of it. Countermeasures involve ducking, then pulling the wire until someone shouts 'Oi!' and applying suitable force of arms. Can be either manpacked (no thanks – or should that be 'no tanks'? [groan]) or vehicle-mounted, which is the infinitely more sensible option. And that's about the lot.

MILAN SPECIFICATION	
Function:	Anti-Tank Missile
Crew:	2
Weight:	7.1kg
Wingspan:	0.26m
Speed:	200m/s (720km/h)
Propulsion:	Solid-fuel rocket
Range:	400–2,000m
Warhead:	Tandem HEAT

CHAINGUN

CHAIN GUN SPECIFICATION	
Calibre:	7.62mm x 51 Nato
Action:	Electrically driven
Rate of fire:	520 – 550 rounds per minute
Muzzle velocity:	862 m/s
Feed system:	Disintegrating link belt

Chain Gun

The greatest contributor to British military casualty figures since Haig's Chief of Staff misunderstood the General's morale-boosting idea of a 'Song and Dance' and instead initiated the shockingly wasteful Somme Advance in 1916. This thing breaks, it burns, it bites, it runs away and it explodes, all without a single round going anywhere near the target. Either the man who invented it was being noshed off at the time, or he was just having a bit of a laugh.

Don't laugh: faults in the Warrior electrical system mean that these things will fire all by themselves, and the way it's mounted in the Challie 2 means that you can't properly aim it, or see where the rounds are going, at ranges below 200 metres. Both of these faults have led to serious 'friendly fire' casualties.

Actually, it was designed as a gravity-fed weapon, but some halfwit at the MoD put it in the Warrior upside down so that the link took all the strain. Probably looked at the link and thought that he could save some pennies there so made it thinner and easily bendable. So what is a spectacularly reliable weapon in US service is generally regarded as a bit of a liability by us Brits. You're better off throwing your helmet at the advancing hordes . . . either that or finding the girl (one hopes) who was giving the nosh and getting one yourself.

MACHINE GUNS

GPMG

The General Purpose Machine Gun can be used either as a light weapon, mounted on a bipod, or in a sustained fire role, mounted on a tripod and fitted with the C2 optical sight. In this role it is operated by a two-man team, grouped in a specialist machine gun platoon to provide battalion-level fire support. Versions of the GPMG are mounted on most Army vehicles and some helicopters.

It is a little-known fact that sustained-fire crews are selected after careful consideration of their medical records, and in particular X-rays of their heads, which must be thick enough to withstand tripod 'grazing' while getting among a bit of man-portability.

MINIMI SPECIFICATION	
Calibre:	5.56 × 45mm NATO
Weight:	6.85kg
Feed:	Belt (220-round) or FNC 30-round magazine
Effective range:	400m
Rate of fire:	700–800 rounds/min

Minimi

Brother of Maximi? The small bloke from *Austin Powers*? Nope, it's a light machine gun, designed and built by FN Herstal in Belgium. Basically a scaled-down GPMG, it performs the job of LMG with a 5.56 round instead of a 7.62 one. Two versions are used in the UK: the regular fixed-stock version and the Para version, which has a collapsible stock and a shorter barrel. Respectively known as the L108A1 and the L110A1.

MORTAR

L16 81MM MORTAR SPECIFICATION	
Weight:	35.3kg
Barrel length:	1.27m
Crew:	3
Calibre:	81mm
Bomb weight:	4.3kg
Rate of fire:	Up to 20 rounds per minute
Range:	5750m

L16 81mm Mortar

The L16 81mm Mortar is the infantry battalion's only exclusive method of indirect fire support (ooooh, get me). Support companies usually have between six and eight mortar detachments, or in the case of the TA between three and six. The HE round has a lethal area of 40 metres and a danger area of 190 metres. The smoke round is white phosphorus and can be used as anti-personnel or incendiary . . . so laugh that one off if you're on the receiving end. The current Illum round is – a kind of mega-firework – one million candle power. The maximum rate of fire for the mortar is up to twenty rounds per minute, but the more common maximum rate of fire is twelve rounds per minute (cutbacks on ammo FFS!).

It has three main parts, the baseplate (the round sticky-in-the-ground thingy), the barrel (commonly called a tube by fecking mongo orifices and Yanks) and the bipod (sticky-outy leg thingy complete with spinny wheels and blood blister-giving clamp device), and is fitted with the C2 sight Trilux (the looky-downy-doesn't-work-in-the-dark bit). It fires three types of ammunition: HE (you must know what that is), WP (that's smoke for the biffs among us) out to a range of 5,650 metres, and Illum (ooh, luk at de pritty lights!) to a range of 4,800 metres.

It is crewed by three and transportable by these means: manpack (yeah right, just bungee this barrel and two greenies, or ammo containers, on the back of your already stupidly heavy FOGB bergen for the next 15km tab, OK mate?), RB44 (gay French Renault Truck Utility Horrendous),Pinzgauer (Gucci Kraut airborne wagon), or in the mech role in the jolly old FV432(m).

SA80 Rifle SPECIFICATION	
Calibre:	5.56mm
Weight:	4.98kg (with loaded magazine and optical sight)
Barrel length:	518mm
Muzzle velocity:	940m/s
Feed:	30-round magazine
Effective range:	400m (600m for section fire)
Cycle rate of fire:	610–775 rounds per minute

SA80

When it first appeared, the SA80 rifle was widely derided as useless. It was called the 'Civil Servant' rifle: you couldn't fire it and it never worked. The plastic 'furniture' was fragile and broke off at inopportune moments, it was highly prone to stoppages, it was heavy and unbalanced, and it could only be used right-handed.

That's bollocks, we were told by the powers that be, it's one of the most accurate service rifles in use anywhere and perfectly reliable if it's properly looked after, so shut the fuck up.

Then came Gulf War 1. Oops. An official inquiry afterwards noted that the 'SA80 did not perform reliably in the sandy conditions of combat and training. Stoppages were frequent despite the considerable and diligent efforts to prevent them. It is extremely difficult to isolate the prime cause of the stoppages. It is, however, quite clear that infantrymen did not have CONFIDENCE in their personal weapon.'

So it was back to the old drawing board. Heckler and Koch, the German arms manufacturer, won the contract to sort out the SA80 and it was reborn – to much scepticism – as the SA80A2. Oddly enough, this time they got it right, more or less. It can still only be fired from the right shoulder (try it from the left and it ejects hot cartridge cases straight into your face), but the reliability issues have been sorted to the extent that it considerably outperforms most other military rifles, including the American M16A4.

Of course, UKSF don't use it because it ~~isn't ally enough~~ isn't ambidextrous; they favour the Diemaco C8 and various other weapons. If you've got it, flaunt it baby!

There are two further variants of the SA80 in use with the British Army: the LSW, which was originally designed as a support weapon but now designated as a marksman's weapon because of its exceptional accuracy; and the carbine version, a sawn-off SA80, for issue to tank crews.

PERSONAL

Not so very long ago a pistol was an essential part of every officer's accoutrement. A Chief Constable would routinely issue a firearms certificate to anyone with the Queen's Commission who wanted to purchase his own sidearm, and if he chose not to, the Army would lend him a Webley, Smith and Wesson or Enfield revolver, which many would retain after their service as a keepsake and souvenir. These were tremendously handy for executing the gardener after he'd been caught rogering the memsahib, or indeed blowing one's own brains out in the wood-panelled library after jacking the children's entire inheritance on Thai ladyboys. Sadly, those days are long gone. Since WW2, pistols have, by and large, been fading into obscurity and obsolescence outside certain specialist areas.

Browning Hi Power

Standard sidearm of the UK military. This pistol of Belgian manufacture is a refinement of John Moses Browning's earlier Colt M1911 pattern service pistol – the good ole Colt .45. The Browning is reliable, without being particularly Gucci, but it does the job. It uses 9mm ammunition, has a single-action trigger and is thirteen-round magazine-fed.

A very decent pistol when it was unveiled in 1935, and though getting long in the tooth it's still effective. New ones bought from the late 1980s onwards have an ambidextrous safety-catch and better contoured grips. Those in danger of actually using these in combat often buy Pachmayr rubber grips and swap them for the hard plastic-issue grips. (Hint: don't lose the issue grips, you'll annoy your armourer.)

PERSONAL

SIG

Based on the fact that they ~~love to have flash guns~~ need modern, functional weaponry to give them an edge over the enemy, the SAS and various other units which tend to get higher civilian clothes allowances have adopted the Swiss/German SIG family of pistols.

These are the firearms equivalent of the Swiss watch, although not actually manufactured in Switzerland. Due to some pesky laws that limit the supply of weapons outside Switzerland, SIG entered into a partnership with Sauer & Sohn, a German firm, since Germany really doesn't mind who they supply weapons to. The upshot being that the rest of the world can get their hands on a rather nicely designed range of small arms safe in the knowledge that they have been manufactured with a Teutonic obsession with detail.

SIG pistols have no safety; instead they offer a de-cocking lever that allows the user to lower the hammer safely once made ready. The pistol can then be carried in perfect safety until required, when a long squeeze of the trigger works the pistol in double action, subsequent shots being single action as normal (a double-action-only version is available, usually for people with an eye to the legal implications of shooting other people).

As a result of their popularity with our covert warriors, the natural home of the SIG pistol is snugly nestled between the waistband of a pair of Diesel jeans and Calvin Klein jockey shorts. The small but perfectly formed P230 in 9mm Short/380ACP is available for the summer months when the larger P226 or P229 models would spoil the line of that classic retro T-shirt.

7 Rifles

Reading, Oxford, Milton Keynes, Mayfair and West Ham are the locations for 7 Rifles, the second TA battalion.

THE SPECIAL AIR SERVICE

The Regiment; the Sarse; the Flat-Heads; the Blades; the Jedi

Sometimes counted as part of the infantry and sometimes as a 'combat arm' in its own right, the SAS has probably been the best-known regiment in the British Army since the May Bank Holiday in 1980 when their assault on the Iranian Embassy was broadcast live around the world. Although it claims to be a small, tightly knit regiment, it must actually be massive in order to have accommodated all the people who claim to have served in it.

There are three regiments of SAS – one regular and two TA – plus the new Special Reconnaissance Regiment (the SRR) and various bolt-on extra bits. Everyone serving with the SAS gets to wear the famous sandy-coloured beret but you only get to wear the winged dagger badge and blue stable belt if you've passed the course, and that's the difficult bit.

Don't mess with the SAS! Sadly, details of most of what the SAS actually get up to are highly classified, but a few facts about this secretive regiment can be revealed:

» All UK pubs are required by law to have one alcoholic regular who claims to be a member of the SAS and was Second Man on the Balcony at the Iranian Embassy.

» Andy McNab's real name is Cyril Clunge.

» All British soldiers have a mate who knows McNab and thinks that he's either a good bloke or a tosser.

» All SAS men must now sign a contract agreeing never to disclose anything about their service, never to call any officer 'Sir' and never to trim their moustaches.

» They are vulnerable to kryptonite, but only during a full moon.

» All serving SAS soldiers are discreet, witty, down-to-earth good blokes; none of them are Waltish, swollen-headed, egotistical prima donnas with a hotline to the *Daily Mirror*'s defence correspondent.

» Since *Dog Soldiers* came out, all SAS weapons are loaded with silver bullets in case they meet real werewolves.

» During the Malayan Emergency the SAS were known by the communist guerrillas as 'the Moustaches from Hell'.

» SAS spelt backwards is SAS.

» During the Falklands Conflict the SAS pioneered the use of specially trained exploding penguins.

» Most people in the town of Hereford have eleven toes and can play the theme tune from the film *Deliverance* on the banjo.

» SAS men are trained to eat Ferrero Rocher at ambassadors' receptions without attracting attention.

» The SAS, and their sister organization the SBS, are blamed for the Army-wide shortage of 'Black Nasty', the tape they use to cover their eyes when they see photographers around.

» Members of the SAS never ostentatiously discuss operations in the pubs and clubs around the city of Hereford. I have never heard them do so and would not know what to listen out for either.

Official SAS moustaches

1.

2.

» Teams of four, eight and sometimes twelve guys do not go on the piss and pose around making it obvious just who they are.

» They do not try to out-psyche anybody foolish enough to stare at them and they never ever carry discreet but oh so obvious military hardware that just cannot be obtained anywhere else except from the QM's stores up at the base.

» Contrary to popular belief, SQMS in the SAS do not issue long droopy moustaches along with MP5s. It has to be 'grown', but the moustache will only grow once the trooper has evaded capture for three months or longer.

22 SAS

Based in Credenhill outside Hereford, 22 SAS is the regular regiment. To join, you need to be a serving member of the armed forces (members of the Royal Navy and RAF can apply too) and to pass the six-month-long selection and training process. The first month involves running up and down hills with a large rucksack on your back, followed by specialist skills training, a jungle training exercise, combat survival training and a parachute course if you aren't already para qualified. Members of 22 SAS do volunteer from all over the Army but it's fair to say that the majority are infantry soldiers, and the majority of them come from the Paras.

Passing the selection course doesn't mean you get to put your feet up: life in the regiment is relentless. As a 'blade' you will be away from home much of the time, and the regiment has the divorce rate to prove it. Special Forces pay is a significant benefit, but every penny of it is earned.

21 SAS and 23 SAS

These are the two TA SAS regiments. The selection and training process is similar to that for regular Special Forces but is extended over about eighteen months to reflect the part-time nature. Individuals can join the TA SAS from other parts of the TA or directly from civilian life (although civilians will need to do the TA combat infantryman course). The role is different to 22 SAS: TA SAS personnel are currently being employed in a role similar to the US Green Berets, mentoring and training local forces in operational areas.

21 SAS is based in southern England and South Wales, 23 SAS recruits in northern England and Scotland.

[LIVING THE ARMY LIFE]

COMPO

Not the tedious little twat in *Last of the Summer Wine* but the issued boxed ration packs given out to soldiers when in the field. 24-Hour Ration Packs do the job: they provide you with everything you need to keep yourself fed and watered for a twenty-four-hour period (except for the water). It may not be exactly luxury, but you can't knock the pleasure of chomping on a bar of chocolate on stag at 0300 hrs. They can be eaten hot or cold.

Before compo went all user-friendly, vegetarian and multicultural, there were but four menus: A, B, C and, unsurprisingly, D. These were not for the faint-hearted. Vegetarian? Fuck you, they're all meat. Muslim or Jew? Ha, fuck you! Bacon Grill, Compo Sausage or Baconburgers for every breakfast. Vitamins? Fuck off, pussy, who needs 'em.

The four menus were:

- Beef and Onion;
- Babies' Heads (see page 22);
- Chicken Curry;
- Chicken Supreme (see page 133).

Among the top treats that came with these were Macedoine – a slurry of bits of things that had once been vegetables – Mars bars, Rolos, boilies, dextrose tablets, Rolled Oats, Biscuits AB and oatmeal blocks. Ah, those were the days!

Nowadays, 24-Hour Ration Packs consist of 'boil in the bag' meals which means that the rations can be easily stashed in your kit or pockets taking up very little room – a vast improvement on the old-style ration packs which were very awkward, being all tinned. So how come the old rations tasted better?

SRR

The SRR was formed from the covert units that were created in Northern Ireland for surveillance and agent handling in hostile environments. Volunteers for SRR do the same basic selection course as SAS and SBS volunteers but also their own specialized continuation training. Once through into the unit, they get to wear a pus-greeny grey beret and sexy 'midnight blue' stable belt – phwoooaarr!

A rare image of SRR members in action.

ANY FOOL CAN BE UNCOMFORTABLE . . .

'Paoli's' Essential Guide to the Wearing of the Green

Army stuff – it's great innit? Looking ally and that. But how does it all fit together? What goes in all those exciting pouches and pockets? How do you complete your ensemble so you look like a hollow-eyed Helmand veteran rather than a paintballer, or spazzy extra from *Red Cap*?

For genuine authenticity you should stuff your pockets with porn, crusty bog paper and fag butts picked up during area cleaning. Your webbing will be disassembled and mouldering in the bottom of your locker – where you lagged on it after a heavy night on the Herforder – and missing most of the vital components, which you have either sold, lost or lent to a mate on the JNCO Cadre. Your kit will be immaculately ironed, but washed so rarely that the build-up of dead skin cells and other detritus creates a form of human starch and there's a danger that if the humidity level gets too high it's going to start marching round your bunk on its own. But before you reach that exalted level of authenticity, you need to get locked on to the basics. Who can you trust? A few words to the wise: remember that 'ex-SAS' Adult Instructor in your cadet detachment who told you to always carry a survival kit? He was a Billy Bullshit Walt whose closest brush with the regular Army was going to the Royal Tournament at Earls Court and who's now doing twelve years' hard time in the segregation unit at Strangeways. And that Corporal at the ATR who made you carry a wash kit with a full-size towel and family bar of soap in your belt kit? The wild-eyed look he had wasn't the result of a rough tour in Helmand but because he knew that when he left his house at 0530 hours

Disclaimer

The advice offered relates to training and operations in temperate environments, or Sennybridge at least. The opinions expressed in this piece are not endorsed by HM Armed Forces or any official body. In particular the author would counsel against telling your training screw or section commander 'that's not the way it says to do it in the *Arrse Guide*' as you are likely to end up wearing your scrotum as a hat and picking your nose out of a catalogue.

to take your squad out for an endurance run he was being swiftly replaced by a Kingo Colour Boy, hanging out of his wife's back doors singing 'I feel like chicken tonight'.

So if you're a Crow, Redarse, Nig, spazzy TV extra, or just one of those overexcited dingbats who incessantly posts topics on Arrse like 'Webbing!!!' or 'What do I keep in my ammunition pouches!!?', prepare for enlightenment.

WEBBING (BELT KIT)

Instructions for assembling 90 Pattern webbing (aka Personal Load Carrying Equipment) are contained in Pamphlet No. 2, *Fieldcraft, Battle Lessons and Exercises*. Which you will never see, but at least you now know what to ask for.

Key points to note when assembling your belt kit are:

» Get the belt right first. Before you fit any pouches (Booties call them 'pooches', because they're gay) to the belt, adjust it so that when the buckle is at the front and the belt is snug around your waist the two 'D' rings at the back are aligned centrally. If you can't manage this get a different-sized belt. There are three sizes: fat cnut (86cm), normal (81cm) and skinny dying bastard (71cm). Your Colour Boy will be happy to help.

» Add pouches working from the rear to the front. Ideally you want everything pushed around as far to the rear as you can, leaving your stomach clear so you can lie prone and still access your front (ammunition) pouches, which should be over your hips.

» Attach the rear pouches using just the T bar and Velcro clips, not the webbing loops (DPM versions only). This will enable you to push the pouches closer together and help keep everything pushed around to the rear. Use all the fastenings and loops on the front two pouches, otherwise they will flap around when they are full of ammo and beat you like a cheap steak.

» Attach the bayonet frog edge-on, using a bit of cord looped through two holes made in the webbing with a hot wire. This saves a lot of space on the belt. Don't fit the frog

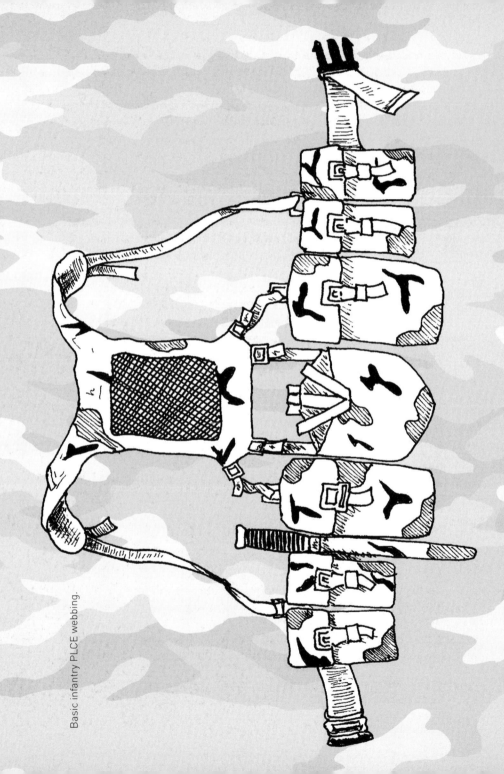

Basic infantry PLCE webbing.

across the back of the yoke, as the bayonet will fall out, and don't fall for the 'you can leave your bayonet in your daysack cos you'll have plenty of warning if you need it' crap. If you're going to do that, why not leave your ammo at home, cos you probably won't need all of it. It's a weapon. Carry it.

» Fit the load spreader ('yoke') to the rear of the belt and adjust it to the right length. Some people prefer to wear their belt higher than others, but it shouldn't be supporting your tits. Loosen the yoke until the belt is somewhere around your waist. Then lock off the straps by feeding them back and forth through the buckle. Adjust the front straps, but don't lock them off as some adjustment will always be necessary. Finally, adjust the lateral load spreader straps and lock them off as with the rear ones. Taping the straps should not then be necessary, but is always popular.

» Thread one utility strap through the small loops on the inner faces of the pouches and adjust it to keep them pulled together and stop them flapping about. Before you do, slip a heavy-duty elastic band (from the vacuum-packed NBC kit packets) around each pouch for attaching scrim to. Some people prefer running a bungee across the outer face of the pouches, through the scrim loops.

Belt Kit Contents

Your belt kit should contain only what you really need to make you effective during dismounted close combat over a period of about twelve to twenty-four hours. You should carry the bare minimum of kit, which basically means ammo, bayonet, digging tool and water, with some food and a layer of clothing to keep you effective overnight or in poor weather. Put less essential items in your daysack (which you can dump if you need to shed weight).

The basic infantry belt kit layout is shown opposite. PONTIs don't get as many pouches, but you get the idea. Don't fit your respirator pouch to your belt: it turns out WMD were a lie, and only government ministers are that fat anyway. Wear it slung round your waist on its strap, if you need it.

Suggested contents for each pouch are as follows, but remember: it all depends on the enemy and the ground, and personal preference. Change the contents to suit the occasion.

1 Left Ammo Pouches

Magazines (generic ammo loads and their distribution can be found in Pamphlet No. 1, *The Infantry Company Group, The Fundamentals*). Weapon cleaning kit (or at least enough of it to carry out cleaning during close operations: oil bottle, pull-through and flannelette. Also have six barrel rods between a fire team, to clear any barrel blockages). Magazine charger (hooked upside-down through the centre loop between the two pouches). Full mags should be placed in top down, so if the lips fail (which will never, ever happen with A2 magazines . . .) the rounds will end up in your pouch, not being sprayed everywhere when you open it. Facing the rounds away from you is probably also good practice.

2 Right Ammo Pouches

Magazines (part of your share from the LSW man's extra ammo) and grenades. (Grenades go in the right ammo pouch because most people will throw them right-handed; mags go in the left pouch because you load left-handed.) Non-infantry personnel should be aware that infantry instructors have strong views on using ammo pouches for items that don't keep your weapon firing. Don't be surprised if your brilliant idea to put your magazines in your bergen to make more room for Haribo is met by a torrent of invective, culminating in you being beaten to death with your own testicles.

3 Bayonet

– in frog fitted edge-on to belt, as described earlier.

4 Waterbottle Pouch

This contains basic 'survival' gear to keep you alive and functioning, if not actually that comfortable, for twenty-four hours. Contains waterbottle (obviously) with NBC cap, sitting in a metal mug (for heating water in). A space blanket is also handy, if not in your smock. Keep a pouched meal and/or brew kit, two hexy blocks and a lighter/matches, all wrapped up in a plastic bag (an MRE packet is ideal), in the small internal pocket (Millbank pocket) as an emergency ration. Water purifying tablets (from the rat packs) go in the little pocket under the top flap of the pouch.

5 ETH (Entrenching Tool Hand) Pouch

If the enemy has a credible indirect fire capability then you need a digging tool with you, on your belt kit. If not, then either replace the ETH pouch with another utility pouch, which you can fill with 'comfort items' or extra ammo as needed, or take the ETH out of the pouch, put your waterbottle in it and use the extra space in your waterbottle pouch. Admittedly the ETH is a pretty shit digging tool, but it is streets ahead of your racing spoon. Talk to a few people who have been under artillery fire for real before you discount it completely.

6 Utility Pouch

This is for whatever you need at the time. Routinely keep your Gore-tex smock, cam cream and snack meal from your rat pack in here, unless you need extra space for anything more relevant to the task you are actually carrying out. You could also keep a small first-aid kit and sewing kit in here (or in your waterbottle pouch). Note that utility pouches can be used as ammo pouches and have the same yoke fittings for this purpose. They are better for carrying belted ammunition and grenades.

7 Helmet (not shown)

You need to be able to clip your helmet to your webbing and get it off again quickly. One option is to fix a '58 Pattern spring-loaded clip (as used to attach the poncho roll) or mini karabiner on to your webbing somewhere, preferably over the utility pouch. You can then clip the helmet on by the rear harness attachment ring. However you do it, avoid the Little Red Riding Hood effect, caused by hanging your helmet from its chinstrap like a picnic basket. Because you will look shit.

8 Respirator Pouch (not shown)

Contents should be as per JSP 410 'Survive To Fight' (current edition). Don't put anything else in the pouch, and don't use a respirator pouch as a 'butt pack'. It is really, really wank.

Avoid the temptation to put extra pouches on the belt, you will just end up carrying non-essential extra weight (if you have room on your belt you probably already are, you fat cunt). Don't tape FFDs to your kit as your webbing will probably be the first thing to be ditched during your initial casevac: why carry a 105kg man out of a killing area when you can drop his kit and carry an 80kg man instead? Name your webbing on the inside face.

The basic combat suit: no soldiers were harmed in the execution of this illustration.

COMBAT KIT

CS95, the multi-layered clothing range which can be worn in various combinations to suit local climatic conditions and the prevailing megalomania of your chain of command.

» The fleece is no longer DPM as it is no longer seen as outerwear (except by really scruffy officers). This is because it has the IRR properties of a Scotsman's arse in a searchlight beam.

» The Gore-tex rain suit is worn over the other stuff to keep it dry. Unless your outer layer(s) is already wet, in which case use the Gore-tex below the wet stuff to stop you getting soaked through to the skin. It may sometimes be worth wearing your Gore-tex under your smock so as to keep access to your pockets, or to protect it from ripping. And, yes, this may cut down on rustling noises; but they will be drowned out anyway by the sound of you crashing about in 25kg of webbing and body armour.

» Don't forget that your body armour, and to some extent your webbing, count as layers, and that your body armour is waterproof.

» The hood of the Gore-tex jacket rolls away into its collar for storage. Roll it away neatly and never, ever wear it, you pikey, civvy, chav, mong. Wearing a hood shuts down most of the senses you need to function effectively on the battlefield, makes you look a cnut, and is only acceptable in extreme weather conditions, such as snow storms, dust storms, clouds of nerve gas or, for members of the RAF, actually having to go outside.

» The 'shirt' is actually called a Lightweight Combat Jacket. It says so on the label. Point this out to anyone who won't let you wear it as an outer layer in the field.

The layer principle means you need to adjust what you are wearing depending on the temperature and how hard you are working. Similarly, adjust the clothing itself to keep a comfortable temperature. The kit is warmer if you close all the openings (neck, cuffs, hem) and items are tucked in to stop the air warmed by your body escaping. If you are overheating, do the opposite: loosen cuffs and roll them back, undo your smock (or just use the Velcro fastenings), loosen off all the draw-cords (which cadets and members of the RLC think have to be used at all times to make a sort of tutu). The point is that it is (mostly) up to you to sort yourself out. Don't mong it and become a heat casualty.

Speaking of mongs, please note: your helmet cover ties at the back. If the draw-cords are at the front, you've got it on back to front and you look a twat.

Everybody's kit looks the same, so mark your surname and last four digits of your Army number on your kit with a permanent marker – inside and somewhere the ink won't soak through (this looks particularly crap on desert kit). Behind a pocket is best. Don't just name the collar tag, as anyone who nicks your kit will just cut it out.

Combat Kit Contents

You should, wherever practical, use your combat jacket/smock as your main shell layer so you always have access to its contents. This saves constantly shifting important items around and inevitably losing them. You should keep the following in your smock:

1 Top Left Smock Pocket

Unless local SOPs say otherwise, this is the immediate aid pocket. Everyone keeps their basic trauma management kit (as opposed to first-aid kit) in this pocket, so everyone knows where to look for it when treating a casualty (use the casualty's own trauma kit to treat them; you might need yours later).

Keep the following in this pocket:

» One or two Emergency Care Bandages (ECB) or First Field Dressings (FFD) (you'll get issued a second on ops, or nick one). If you don't have ECB, carry two elasticized bandages with you as well (somewhere), as these are a far more effective way of applying FFD and direct pressure.

» Combat Application Tourniquet (CAT).

» Morphine autoject, in protective 'coffin'.

» *Battlefield Casualty Drills Aide Memoire* (Army Code 71638).

» Whistle, looped to buttonhole of top flap.

» Under the top flap, mark your surname, zap number and blood group. If you are really keen, sew a strip of white tape on first. Don't write your blood group on your helmet cover, FFD outer or webbing: it looks gay, and the chances of them still being with you at the point you receive whole blood are near zero. The British medical chain will always cross-match before transfusion anyway, so this is just in case. You could end up being cas-evaced by a Coalition ally or, God help you, to a local civilian hospital. In which case every little helps.

2 Top Right Smock Pocket

Keep the following in this pocket:

>> Notebook and pen/pencil in a plastic bag. The issue MoD
notebook – MoD F383A (cover) and F383 (notebook insert) – is
fine, and free from your company clerk. Don't waste money on
'waterproof' notebooks, they're shit. If they get wet the pages fuse
together into a solid lump of plastic which may be waterproof but
is unusable as a notebook.

>> Torch. This should be looped through the buttonhole of the pocket
flap in such a way that it is permanently fastened to you, but can
be unlooped easily if you need to hand it to someone else. Choose
one that uses Army-issue AA batteries. A Maglite is fine in my
view, and it's what you'll be issued on ops, but whatever. Any red
filter must be easily removable: you can't see contours on maps in
red light, however tactical it makes you feel.

3 Left Thigh Pocket

The left thigh ('map') pocket of the trousers is usually used as the
immediate aid pocket if body armour is worn over the smock/lightweight
combat jacket. Same contents as above, less the whistle.

4 Other Pockets

Other pockets should contain the following items which together with everything else in your pockets make up your basic 'survival kit':

>> Bic lighter/matches. Carry lots of cheap lighters as they're better at lighting hexy than matches, and when they run out will still produce a spark capable of igniting the padding in an FFD in a 'survival' situation. Which is gonna happen. No, really.

>> Penknife. Carry this in your trouser pocket, looped to a belt loop by 75cm or so of paracord, again in such a way that it can be easily unlooped. Don't carry your knife in your smock pockets as you tend to use it at waist not face or chest height; and, unless you have always wanted the nickname 'Fingers', do not use bungee cord or anything elastic to tie it on: in wet conditions the knife will be twanged back through your slippery palm, slicing you up like a Kray twin. The knife should be small and robust and have a tin opener (if not, carry a tin opener too). The Army clasp knife is ideal, but rarely gets issued. You could carry a Leatherman instead (issued on ops) but avoid expensive Gucci brands. This is a working knife, not for big-timing it around the council estate.

>> Ear plugs. Handy when you know CAS is on the way.

>> Racing spoon. Plastic for preference, metal is fine, wooden is a health risk. MRE spoons are ideal (carry lots, spread through your kit); the Gucci solution is one of those 'stronger than steel' Lexan jobs.

>> Bog paper, waterproofed (the packs of tissues from the rat packs are ideal). Also, some KFC stylee 'moist towelette' sachets, nicked off the cookhouse table. For polishing around your piles.

>> Some food. Nothing too bulky, heavy or likely to melt/explode. Sweets usually.

>> 15m green string. Opinions vary on exactly how much string you need on you, but some is definitely handy. Comms cord for ambushes, harbour sentries etc. (if needed in the Bowman age) should come from the big roll carried by your Platoon Sergeant,

(4 *Other Pockets cont.*)

so this is just for general use. Use Army-issue 'green hairy', not para cord. You aren't going to want to chop up your precious para cord to help tie up a basha. Alternatively use a small box of dental floss: 100m weighs a few grams, you won't break it, and it won't form a large dark-green bundle of tangle in your pocket. It will also ensure you do not return from an exercise with cavities in your teeth, from eating all those sweets.

5 Other Items
You could also carry:

» Silva compass. If you're going to spend your money on one item of kit, this is the one. It's not sexy, it's not ally, but it is definitely genuine SAS kit. Loop it on to a pocket flap so you don't lose it. Make sure it has graduations marked in mils (unless you are in the RAF, in which case Google 'The Metric System' and 'The 21st Century' and then stop wasting our money on Eurofighters).

» Space blanket. Might be worth having, if it's cold.

Silva Compass – real 'SAS' kit

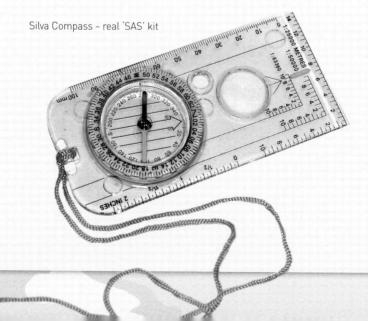

GUCCI KIT

Current British Army clothing and personal equipment is excellent. No joke. There is really no need to buy smocks, webbing, boots; the stuff you get issued does the job well, it's free, and it gets replaced when it wears out. Be honest with yourself. You don't need a Para smock, you want one. Cos it'll make you look ally. The issue CS95 Field Jacket is much better, but people persist in wearing Para smocks. Why? Because it makes them look like members of the Parachute Regiment, and the Parachute Regiment are ally (strangely enough the Parachute Regiment wear them for the same reason, and don't give me that crap about needing the crotch flap, it doesn't stop you jumping in SAS smocks does it?). Boots are about the only item that you could justifiably buy as everyone's feet are different and issue boots are designed for some mythical everyman. Even so, examine your motives carefully. Remember: girls don't like boys, girls like cars and money. Every penny you spend on Army kit is putting you further away from getting laid.

But you're gonna do it anyway, so here's some advice:

Buy Useful Stuff

Silva compasses, a decent pocket knife, pace counters, Ortlieb bags, the components of your first-aid kit – these are all useful. Even US 'tiger's eye' helmet bands, kneepads, headtorches, a spare utility pouch or a decent daysack are improvements to your basic kit. 'Rambo' knives, naff smocks with a million pockets, anything with the words 'survival' or 'special operations' in its name – these are not useful, are usually expensive, and will make you look like a TA storeman.

Boots

Before buying Gore-tex boots, remember they are not waterproof if you kneel in a stream or when rain runs down your legs into the top of them. They do, however, take for fecking ever to dry out once wet. Conversely, Magnums have the waterproof properties of a household sponge, and also take for fecking ever to dry out once wet. Issue Assault Boots are reasonably waterproof and dry out fairly quickly. A spare pair of socks is a lot cheaper than a pair of Lowas.

Buy Issue Kit

Kit that is on issue (but not necessarily to you) will meet proper military specifications, including IRR protection and robustness. This should still hold good for foreign issue kit (although remember some armies will have different imperatives). If you buy Web-tex or other low-spec stuff, you risk nightsights making you glow like a Ukrainian firefighter. The other advantage of (British) issue kit is that if you stay in long enough, you will eventually get a chance to exchange it for free. Which you won't be able to do with your Arktis ops vest.

Buy through the System

British kit can, apparently, be purchased through the system for wholesale prices, according to a letter in *Soldier* magazine. Yeah, right. Still, Col Silas Suchanek of the Defence Clothing Integrated Project Team writes: 'The new Operational Clothing Catalogue (JSP 529) provides details of the full range of operational clothing and includes pictures, sizes, guide prices and wear-and-care instructions. The windproof smock (NSN 8415-99-132-3951) guide price is £36. The mechanisms for soldiers to buy items of combat clothing exist but it is more a question of the chain of command sanctioning such purchases.' In other words, you haven't got a hope. Still, in your own time, go on.

Buy through the system... or wait for someone to issue it to you.

And finally . . .

Think About It. Do without the item of kit you want to buy for a bit and see if you really need or want it. Also, think about what wearing/possessing the item is going to say about you. Wearing a sniper smock when you are not a qualified sniper does not make people think you are a steely-eyed harbinger of death. It makes them think you are a twat.

YOU'RE IN
THE ARMY
NOW

WHO'S WHO

OFFICERS

The role of the officers in the British Army is to act as both leaders and managers of the soldiers they are responsible for, leading them in barracks and in battle, helping to manage their careers and looking after their welfare at all times – all of this in order to bring out the best in them.

Well, supposedly anyway. Officers, like soldiers, come in all shapes and sizes and range from those who are dazzlingly good at their jobs to those who are embarrassingly poor. Despite this, expectations are always high. The Army's officer corps is a pretty strict meritocracy and by and large senior officers are very good at what they do, and they expect the same standards from the junior officers they command. It's a high-pressure career.

Officers come in three broad types:

Direct Entry (DE)

DE officers (generally known as 'Ruperts') get their commissions as the result of passing the Army Officer Selection Board (AOSB) at Westbury and subsequently the Commissioning Course at the Royal Military Academy Sandhurst. Most come direct from civilian life but a minority (often called 'Rodneys', or 'Wodneys', because they come up thwough the wanks) are privates and junior NCOs whose leadership potential has been spotted within their units.

The basic educational requirement is five GCSEs and two A levels, or their equivalent, although about 80 per cent of students attending Sandhurst now also have degrees. Soldiers who pass the AOSB don't necessarily need to have these but if they don't, they get sent on a course to prepare them for the 'academic' demands of Sandhurst.

Late Entry (LE)

Typically, LE officers have served for between eighteen and twenty-two years in the ranks and made it to Warrant Officer before they are selected by their regiment or corps for a commission. They undergo a four-week Late Entry Commissioning Course at Sandhurst and are usually then commissioned as Captains. LE officers have generally seen it all and done it all and can be pretty scary characters for soldiers and junior officers so derisive nicknames aren't common, but it isn't unknown for them to be referred to as 'Reginalds' (and occasionally, by young officers who have just undergone a severe arse-chewing, as 'GOPWOs' – short for Grossly Over Promoted Warrant Officers). In the bad old days, LE officers were pretty much restricted to admin and quartermaster type roles, but nowadays there are much wider employment opportunities for them on the operational side of life as well.

Professionally Qualified Officers (PQOs)

The Army needs medical and dental professionals, vets, lawyers and chaplains who need to be uniformed members of the armed forces but don't necessarily need to go through the full one-year DE Commissioning Course. Qualified personnel go through a selection board, the four-week PQOs course at Sandhurst (known as the 'Vicars and Tarts' course), followed by training in their professional speciality. The PQOs course is designed to teach PQOs about the values and standards of the Army, basic military skills, living in the field and how to wear and look after their uniforms, although many PQOs seem to have slept through this bit.

Sandhurst instructors: forget daleks, vampires and werewolves, these men are really scary.

It wasn't that long ago – in the big scale of things – that if you weren't the product of a reasonably decent public school, you didn't have a prayer of being commissioned (as a direct entrant, at least) into the cavalry, Guards and some of the grander line infantry regiments, no matter how good you happened to be at the job. Indeed, the expected lifestyle that a young officer was supposed to maintain in some regiments was so lavish that it was unimaginable that their officers would be able to live off their salaries alone.

Is this still true? Nope, not at all, and anyone who claims it is is either a bullshitter or talking out of their arse. Since the end of WW2 social barriers have been coming down faster than a QA's thong. Don't believe this? Take a look at the Sandhurst graduation lists which get printed in *The Times*, the *Telegraph* and the *London Gazette*, which still include the previous schools and universities of the graduates. For each newly minted Second Lieutenant who went to Eton you are likely to find ten or twenty whose alma mater was the Nelson Mandela Community School in Byker, or its near equivalent. Regional accents are now the norm, ethnic minorities common, and chins more or less obligatory.

What the modern-day British Army is looking for is whether you are up to the job and whether or not you will fit in.

HOW DO I JOIN AS AN OFFICER?

Go along to your local Armed Forces Careers Information Office or register your interest via the Army Jobs website and you'll soon receive an invitation to come and have a chat with an Army Careers Adviser (Officers). He or she will be making an initial sift to ensure that you have sufficient educational qualifications, are the right nationality, possess the correct number of arms, legs, ears, eyes and so forth, and are not a habitual criminal. They will also make a rough assessment of whether they think you have the potential to be an Army officer (hint: nineteen hours a day playing World of Warcraft won't cut it). This means that they want to see that you are reasonably physically fit, intelligent and take an informed interest in the world around you.

Although it will seem relatively informal, your visit to the office is the first step in a job application process, so treat it as such. Dress smartly and think about why you want to join the Army. Don't bullshit: if you aren't spotted right away, any untruths you come out with will be picked up on at some stage during the process and you will have to account for them. The Army isn't looking for a stereotype, it's looking for any person with the potential to be an effective leader of its soldiers. Have a look at the jobs website and think about which career paths might interest you. And remember, you're selling yourself!

If this chat goes well, you will be

given a sheaf of forms to fill out and send back to the ACA(O) and he or she will book you on to an AOSB briefing and perhaps also send you on some 'familiarization' visits to the regiments and corps you've expressed an interest in. But the big hurdle now is the Army Officers Selection Board at Westbury, which takes place in two basic parts.

The Briefing

This takes place at Westbury over two days, and gives applicants the chance to:

>> Attempt the multi-stage fitness test, alias the bleep test. This involves running up and down a short course, turning in time to a series of bleeps which get closer and closer together.

>> Take part in leaderless command tasks. These are the classic 'you have a plank, two barrels and a toggle rope, now get across this crocodile-infested river' exercises. These show whether you can lead and be led, and work as an effective member of a team.

>> Be interviewed. Short interviews with various members of the AOSB.

>> Sit a psychometric test which will hopefully weed out any serial killers who are too stupid to see through psychometric tests (for example, the correct answer to a poser like 'I really want to kill my father so I can spend more time sodomizing my mother' is likely to be 'e. strongly disagree').

>> Go through a planning exercise. This is a paper exercise which will involve calculating speed, time and distance factors, and selecting the best course of action from several alternatives.

>> Attempt an individual assault course, running around and leaping over a number of small obstacles, trying to do as many as possible in a set time.

>> Take part in group discussions, designed to see whether you can articulate your thoughts clearly and assertively, as well as accept the opinions of others and adapt your views when necessary.

After this, the AOSB makes a judgement on how likely a candidate is to pass and issues one of the following grades:

1	Crack on, you're ready to do AOSB whenever you want.
2–6	You should be ready to do AOSB in six months if you work on certain problem areas.
2–12	You should be ready to do AOSB in twelve months if you work on certain problem areas.

3 You will probably always be borderline. Have a good think about whether you want to do it at all.

4 AOSB is not for you.

Main Board

When you're through the briefing, and hopefully clutching a grade 1 pass, the next thing to think about is AOSB Main Board. This is a three-day process, starting on Monday afternoon and finishing on Thursday morning. On arrival the candidates become mere numbers and colours, designated by the bibs they are given. And then they get stuck into a series of tests similar to those on the briefing, but also including:

>> leading command tasks;

>> more interviews;

>> current affairs tests;

>> a five-minute 'lecturette' on a subject which is given to you by the DS.

At the end of the Main Board there is a formal dinner in the Candidates'

Mess – the first time (allegedly) when the candidates aren't under supervision and are allowed to relax. Classic (and probably apocryphal) stories abound of indiscretions committed on the dinner night, e.g. a female candidate discovered by one of the staff being spit-roasted on the pool table in the mess bar. It's best to avoid getting too pissed, whether you're up for a spit-roast or not, because the final event on Thursday morning is a group obstacle race.

At the end of all this it's pass or fail. If you pass, even if you're borderline, you've won a place at Sandhurst (the old system for borderline candidates involved Rowallan Company at Sandhurst, a brutal and fearsome twelve-week beasting session designed as a 'character-building' process); if you fail, they'll either suggest you have another go after a set period, or advise you to look elsewhere for a career.

How to Pass

AOSB isn't really a test you can swot for because much of it is about identifying innate leadership potential. What you can do is:

>> Get fit. You don't need to be an Olympic athlete, you just need to be able to pass the relatively easy physical tests you're set.

» Get clued up about the Army. Reading this book is an excellent start, but find a few books on recent British military operations and read them too.

» Get clued up on current affairs. Read a serious newspaper; read magazines like the *Economist*, *Spectator*, *New Statesman* and *Private Eye*; watch the news on TV rather than *Emmerdale*.

» Don't pose as something you aren't. The Army isn't about social class. Nobody cares if your mum's a cleaning lady or if she's a duchess, and you'll be found out if you try to fake it.

» Put maximum effort into everything you do.

SANDHURST

The Royal Military Academy Sandhurst is like a minor public school where the CCF has got out of control, or, alternatively, it's 'arguably the finest officer training establishment in the world' (it's definitely the finest officer training establishment in Camberley). Over the course of forty-two weeks divided into three terms of fourteen weeks each, officer cadets receive basic military training combined with leadership, management and administrative training. Infantry platoon tactics are used as the basic medium for leadership training but everyone who passes the course then goes on to do specialized training with their own arm or corps.

Sandhurst itself is located in Camberley, on the border between Surrey and Berkshire. It consists of two very beautiful buildings, Old College and New College, together with a number of somewhat less attractive buildings, set in a large area of landscaped parkland adjacent to the Barossa Common training area (as seen in the film *Gladiator*) and the Broadmoor secure loony bin. Among the great joys of Sandhurst are its traditions. These include a first day when hordes of clean-cut young men and women turn up with their parents, clutching suitcases, trunks and ironing boards, are shown to their rooms by a very polite Colour Sergeant, and then take tea with their company staff. This is rather like the

Pace-sticking: a minority sport.

DEXTROSE TABLETS

A tube of these used to appear in every ration pack. Essentially weapons-grade Trebor Refreshers, these were used to deliver sugar – and thus calories – to the field soldier at the cost of an acidic aftertaste that made one's eyes revolve in different directions. Now superseded by compo boilies.

'hypnotism' practised by mongooses before they scoff a snake. As soon as the parents are off the premises, the smiles disappear to be replaced by snarled abuse and ferocious beastings.

The Commissioning Course

Organizationally, officer cadets are divided into companies, with three companies of three platoons per intake. There are three intakes per year, in September, January and May, and each intake will in turn be the junior, intermediate and senior division. The companies are commanded by a Major, with a 2ic and three platoon commanders who are Captains. Each company also has a WO2 Company Sergeant Major (the officer cadets call him 'Sir', and he calls them 'Sir'; the difference is that they mean it and he doesn't) and four Colour Sergeants (one each for the platoons and one CQMS).

Junior Term

The first term is all about basic training: lots of drill; lots and lots of PT; weapon training; signals; first aid; navigation; individual fieldcraft; and, of course, what amounts to a Master's degree in polishing boots and shoes. The first five weeks are notoriously tough, with officer cadets averaging about four hours' sleep per night, no opportunities for relaxation and every supposedly spare moment filled with kit cleaning and sport.

Intermediate Term

The intermediate term is theoretically more classroom-based than the junior term, focusing on tactics, staffwork, administration and military law. Nevertheless, PT and drill continue at full steam ahead, together with shorter tactical exercises. It also features the regimental selection board, so make sure you work your little green socks off in the junior term.

Senior Term

This is the culmination of the course and includes several longer exercises and the Sovereign's Parade. By now, officer cadets are expected to be more self-motivated and 'beastings' are fewer, nevertheless there is plenty of opportunity for things to go wrong.

The pace of the Commissioning Course is unrelenting: there's a lot to pack in to a relatively short period – up until the early 1970s the course was two years long – and officer cadets are being assessed continually. Anyone falling behind will be placed on a series of warnings ranging from a 'Platoon Commander's warning' (the least serious) to a 'College Commander's warning', which is not far off being a death knell. If these don't work, cadets can be either 'back-termed' – i.e. made to repeat a term – or even binned from the course entirely.

The Commissioning Course is very physical and this does take its toll on some officer cadets. Problems often include ankle, knee and back injuries from doing PT, as well as other injuries resulting from training accidents. Those who pick up injuries which prevent them from continuing their training are 'Y listed', which is in effect a medical 'back-terming' in order to give the cadet a chance to recover. Oddly enough, an officer cadet who was accidentally shot by a Colour Sergeant with a 66mm anti-tank rocket in the mid-eighties did complete the course!

Progress in the Commissioning Course is measured in various ways. Apart from the basic tests of military training, like the Combat Fitness Test, Weapon Handling Tests, Personal Weapons Tests and so on, the Commissioning Course has various 'officer specific' testing components, including 'PRACTAC' (the practical tactics test) and MK1. These are designed to demonstrate that officer cadets have absorbed the

Talking tactics.

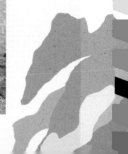

tactics and doctrine they have been taught both in classroom lectures and while on exercise in the field. Probably more important, however, is the system of exercise command appointments. In every phase of each field training exercise one member of each platoon is appointed platoon commander, one becomes the platoon sergeant, others are appointed section commanders, 2ics, and so on. This gives the DS the chance to see how officer cadets, who might be dazzling in the classroom when everything is warm and cosy, operate when they haven't slept for two days, it's pissing down with rain and they've got raging constipation from eating compo rations.

The culmination of the course is normally a two-week final exercise which used to take place somewhere warm and exotic, like Cyprus, but nowadays, for cost reasons, is more likely to happen at Sennybridge in Wales. This will involve company-level operations as well as a 'final attack' by the whole course, during which, by tradition, the officer cadets get to wear their regimental headgear for the first time. It's a moment of elation as the re-org after the attack will generally include generous quantities of champagne – but it's worth remembering that the final 'binning' session takes place at the end of this final exercise and some of the officer cadets will be back-termed or even hoofed out completely.

Choice of Regiment

Most officer cadets have a fairly clear idea of which regiment or corps they want to join when they arrive at Sandhurst. The familiarization process for potential officers typically involves visits to a number of different regiments, and often applicants will have family or local connections anyway. Even so, final regimental destination is not decided until the intermediate term.

The process is fairly straight-forward. Officer cadets indicate which regiment or corps they want to commission into at the beginning of the course. Thereafter, the regimental 'reps' at Sandhurst keep an eye on their progress. In theory, if a cadet has done well enough and there are sufficient vacancies, everyone should get their first choice.

In practice, of course, it's slightly different. Some regiments and corps are very oversubscribed (the Parachute Regiment, the Household Cavalry, the Guards, the Gurkhas, the Army Air Corps, the Intelligence Corps) and the less able candidates for these will be gently prodded in the direction of other parts of the Army. Thus a good officer cadet who isn't quite up to the standard for the Paras might well find himself commissioned into his 'local' infantry regiment. On the other hand, a few corps tend to be undersubscribed – the RLC, the AGC and the RAMC particularly – and often officer cadets who for one reason or another don't get their first or second choice find

Sovereign's Parade: a tri-annual festival of boot polishing and bullshit.

themselves railroaded in. It isn't the end of the world – transfer between regiments and corps after commissioning is certainly possible – but it can be disappointing.

The Sovereign's Parade

The culminating event of the Commissioning Course is the Sovereign's Parade, a grand occasion which takes place on the Old College Square to which one can invite parents, girlfriends, boyfriends, husbands, wives and children. It's normally presided over by a senior politician, a visiting foreign head of government or state, a member of the royal family, and occasionally by the Queen herself. This is followed by a very civilized luncheon, the handing back of a lot of superfluous kit, the packing up of rooms and, in the evening, the commissioning ball, a drunken debauch designed to test newly delivered regimental mess kit to the limit.

It Ain't Over Yet . . .

You've finished Sandhurst and now you're a fully trained officer, right? Sorry, there's a way to go yet. You'll normally get a week or so of leave after Sandhurst before you have to report to your new regiment or corps, and the chances then are that after a short introductory period you'll be whisked away to do your 'special-to-arm' training – learning the skills needed to actually lead members of your chosen regiment or corps. Thus newly minted Gunner officers head off to do their YOs course at Larkhill, infanteers head for PCBC at Brecon, tankies go to Bovington, and so on.

OFFICERS

BILL TRENCH

When he was RSM of the 1st Battalion, the favourite part of Bill Trench's week was Friday afternoon when the Warrant Officers' and Sergeants' Mess would hold a 'happy hour' to which they would generally invite the CO, the Adjutant, a couple of Company Commanders and a few of the Captains and Lieutenants. Bill would make sure that none of the officers ever had to pay for a drink, that the bar snacks were replenned and the finger-pointing never got excessively aggressive. It was, he felt, the perfect way to demonstrate that it was his Mess which was the real engine room of the battalion, not the Officers' Mess.

And even now he's crossed the divide and accepted his late entry commission, he still feels exactly the same. He could have gone back to the battalion in a QM role but instead he decided to go for the SO3 G1 job at a regional brigade HQ not far from his home town in the Midlands. In the first instance, it's the first time that he and Muriel have ever been able to live in the house they'd bought nine years before; and secondly, he wouldn't have felt comfortable being back at the battalion as an officer, working with men he'd known for twenty-odd years but with a fundamentally changed relationship.

Plus – and he never thought he'd say this – he doesn't really miss it. Working at brigade is an 8.30 to 5 job 90% of the time and he really doesn't resent the occasional Saturday away visiting a TA unit. He can spend his weekends in the garden or walking the dogs with Muriel and the kids. Happy days.

With five years to go before retirement from the Army, Bill's plan is to try to sort himself out with a job in Defence Estates at one of the local training areas. He knows the ground, he knows the personalities and he could sort the admin out standing on his head. Definitely something to look forward to.

GUY FRIEND

Everyone likes Guy. He's physically fit, conscientious, witty and kind, but perhaps not as bright and sparky as some of his contemporaries. Even so, he's widely regarded as a safe pair of hands for organizing events like the Officers' Mess Summer Ball.

This isn't quite why he joined the Army: at his independent day school he was senior cadet in the CCF and he got himself commissioned in the OTC when he was doing his politics and geography degree at Leeds University. At that time he saw himself as a future David Stirling or Fitzroy MacLean. Instead, it turned out that what he was really good at was admin and organization. He isn't afraid to think outside the box, it's just that other people do it better than he does.

So instead of dashing, he's settled on a traditionalist image with just a hint of extroversion to show he's not a total clone. What he'd really like to

do is command his regiment but he can see this isn't going to happen: the best jobs seem to go to people who've served in the airborne or commando brigades. He'll make his half Colonel if he stays in, but he's thinking about getting out at the initial pension point.

Which will be a shame, because he'll miss the lads. He was a bit nervous of commanding soldiers when he was first commissioned but it turned out that most of them were pretty normal boys and girls really. They do some stupid things from time to time – sorting out the Gunner who'd bought a BMW on HP on a £14k salary springs to mind – but mostly they work hard and get on with the job. They like him too: he doesn't shout and swear, and though he's a stickler for getting the job done, they know where they stand with him.

All the lads assume that Captain Guy is going to marry some horsey Caroline type, but Guy's found love and happiness with a physiotherapist called Kate and after they're married, they're planning to get a quarter in Paderborn while he does his Battery Commander job. After that, who knows? Guy's thinking about commuting his pension, doing a proper MBA and moving into management consultancy. Kate wants kids and wants to live in the country. So that'll be nice: Guy already does some voluntary stuff with the regimental association, so he can stay in touch with the Army that way: who knows, after a couple of years he might make a comeback with CVHQ?

JIM CHIPPER

Jim's first job in the Army after trade training was in a Brigade HQ but back then he was a Lance Jack in the MI Section and spent much of his time putting up tents, gluing maps together and logging contact reports as they came in over the net. Now, as SO2 Plans, he's basically the number two after the COS – on the G2/G3 side at least – and this could be a stepping stone for greater things. A Major in the Royal Horse Artillery with a Masters in Defence Administration – not bad for a Geordie who left school with five GCSEs!

Jim hated the A3 when he did it, in one of the last squads to go through Ashford, but getting out to Germany afterwards had been fantastic, a real eye-opener for a young lad who'd barely been out of the country before. He'd been marked out as potential officer material not long after and within two years of leaving Ashford he was back in training at Sandhurst on the DE commissioning course.

He'd been in the middle third at Sandhurst, about where you'd expect a bright non-grad commissioning from the ranks to be, and while he'd looked at a couple of infantry regiments, his ultimate choice had come down to Gunners or RLC. He'd gone with the Gunners because he thought it would be more of a challenge. Good choice.

The only real mistake he'd made at this stage was marrying Janine, his girlfriend from Ponteland. She was a lovely lass, but got dreadfully homesick and never fitted in with the other wives on the patch at his first regiment in Germany. They tried to make it work, but eventually he came home from an Uhlan Eagle to find she'd gone home to her mum. The regiment had been great about it and had given him time off to try to sort things out but it didn't happen. Good thing they didn't have kids. According to Jim's mum, Janine remarried a local government officer from Newcastle and has settled down with a couple of bairns, so it worked out all right for her.

Wife number two was a Captain in the AGC (ETS) when Jim met her in Prizstina while he was doing an SO3 tour. They hit it off right away and the great thing is she knows the score. One way or another they spent most of the late 1990s and 2000s in the Balkans and Iraq on various op tours, but they've still managed to have two great kids, Max and Daisy, and to keep their careers going, although Cath is thinking she'll take her pension in the next couple of years and try to get into teaching in the UK. It might be a chance for them to buy somewhere half decent.

Jim's a straightforward kind of bloke. He'll knock heads together when he needs to, but as long as the work gets done properly, he's happy. The SO3s all think that, unlike the COS, he has actually managed to hang on to his sense of humour. Oddly enough, the Geordie accent has almost disappeared now and lots of the young officers are surprised to discover that Jim used to be an NCO. The future looks good for Jim and Cath. He'll get his half Colonel and some kind of command is not impossible, but he's a steady pair of hands and just the kind of chap for longer-term procurement projects. Who would have thought it?

MARCUS FRIGHTE

Marcus is pretty pissed off that the Army are holding him to the full notice period. It isn't like they were going to let him stay anyway. Pig reckons that a lot of the hedge funds are hiring now, which is great, and that they'd definitely be interested in someone with a decent enough degree and four years as a regular officer – well three if you don't count Sandhurst. Apparently, they cream themselves over guys with military experience, and Marcus can tell them about his six months in Afghan as the regimental assistant IO. I mean, if they cream over the Army, what will they think about intelligence, right?

He'd be in a pretty good position even if he wasn't ex-Army, because he's public school and his third from Durham is easily worth a 2.1 or a first from one of these ex Polys, so that's cool. The career change is pretty straightforward: he never meant to stay past the basic three year short service commission, I mean, who would? All the greatest Generals leave as Captains: everyone knows that.

Ma and Pa are cool that Marcus is getting out too. Pa's business is holding its own, and maybe he'll work there for a bit while he gets something lined up in the City. Actually, being the assistant adjutant is pretty cool because he's getting a lot of admin experience that he just wouldn't have got if he was still a Troop Commander.

At Sandhurst they said you would have to rely on your Troop Sergeant and the NCOs, but Marcus's just seemed to drop him in the shit the whole time. He never gave them a hard time for being late, so why did they get so chippy about it when he was late in a few times on a Monday: it's a four-hour drive from Fulham to Catterick on a good day and if you hit roadworks, you're really up shit creek. Anyway, that was pretty disloyal … and so was refusing to go on patrol with him in Helmand. Marcus didn't like the way the squadron leader took Sergeant Jacobs' word against his; who was Jacobs to say he was dangerous?

Anyway, the plan is to give the regimental run on Friday afternoon a miss, and try to hit the Hollywood Arms off the Fulham Road with Pig before it gets too crowded, then maybe onto Bouji. Should be a laugh.

RAV CHANDRA

The Army sees Rav Chandra as some kind of poster-boy for ethnic minority access; he sees that as a bit tragic. Sure, his grandparents originally immigrated from India but that was just after the Second World War, and it was so that his grandfather could take over a chair in Civil Engineering at the university in London, not run a corner-shop in Peckham, for Christ's sake. Rav's dad is a consultant surgeon in the NHS; his mum runs her own PR company; and they're all living very comfortably in one of the leafier parts of Ealing in west London, thanks very much.

Rav decided on the Army when he was in the sixth form at St Paul's in Barnes and getting a bit pissed off with the occasional sly dig about being 'Indian'. It turned out to be a somewhat effortless process: AOSB was pretty straightforward with no dramas and he was straight into an Army Bursary for his three years at Cambridge.

No question Sandhurst was tough, but Rav was a solid top-third all the way through and had no problems walking into the regiment of his choice. Cavalry surprised a few people, but so what? One of the advantages of his ethnic background is he doesn't have to dress in the ridiculous tweedy clobber his contemporaries feel obliged to don: he isn't pretending to be a Shropshire landowner.

The plan is to push out five years and leave at twenty-seven. Vicky, the girlfriend he met in his first year at Cambridge, will have qualified as a doctor by then and Rav is looking at the City or perhaps an executive role in one of the bigger PMCs. He'll make up his mind closer to the time. The Army has been good to Rav, but he never saw it as a long-term career. Politics is where Rav's interests lie, and a stint as a Cavalry officer, together with his impeccable education and his ethnic background, will be a potent combination in the modern Conservative Party. The plan is to be in the House of Commons by the age of thirty-five, and after that, who knows?

RUPERT THRUSTE-WRIGHT

Since he took over as Brigade COS, Rupert has made it his business not to suffer fools gladly – or at all if they're sufficiently weak to allow him to get away with it. He wants Brigade HQ to be poised, agile and ready to deal with anything that the Brigadier, ISAF or even the Taliban can throw at it. Don't get in his way or you'll get hurt! Brigade HQ is a monument to manoeuvrism, almost as much as Rupert's career.

Rupert's dad, Colonel Mike Wright, started out as a Driver in the RCT in the early seventies, before getting picked up for Sandhurst and a commission in the Royal Signals. He married Rupert's mum, QA Captain Deirdre Thruste, when they were serving together in Rinteln. Rupert spent most of his childhood at boarding schools in south-west England, only seeing the family during school holidays at their various quarters across Germany in the good old days of BAOR. Mum and Dad retired to Somerset when Rupert was reading Business Studies at Kingston University (where he reinvented himself as Thruste-Wright) and he's hoping that if he gets the kids into prep schools down that way they'll be able to keep an eye on things for him and Shona.

Rupert knew from the first day he arrived at Sandhurst that he was going to fight his way to the top. He always made sure he was up at the front on runs; always made sure that the DS saw him helping his weaker comrades in their command appointments; and always made sure they knew that he was just as exasperated as they were that some cadets weren't prepared to make as much effort as he was to get 9 Platoon to the top. Halfway through his first term he ditched his original plan to follow Dad into the Royal Sigs and went inf instead. The platoon commander seemed chuffed that Rupert was keen on his own regiment! It's all been good ever since. Failing selection in the jungle was a disappointment, but he got a pretty decent write-up and had a mega-tour as an SO3 in 16 Air Assault instead, which got him his wings at least. Shriv was hard work but a blast; company command a breeze, though Iraq had quietened down too much for him to really shine by then. A gong would have been nice.

He met Shona in a pub off the Fulham Road on a night out from Colchester. She was working for Foxton's and flat-sharing in Putney with a couple of school friends. She's taken to Army life like a duck to water – her parents run a property business in Spain, so she's used to moving around – and while Rupert's on tour they've agreed that she'll be looking for a buy-to-rent property so they can generate some extra income. Shona was fine when Rupert was in Iraq, and he can't see her having a problem while he's in Afghan. He'll be relatively safe in Brigade HQ after all.

THRUSTE-WRIGHT

Rupert's got a slight idea he might be getting jiggy with SO3 Legal at some stage. She looks like she might be persuaded. It won't be a problem: she'll understand that what happens on tour, stays on tour.

So the future looks bright. If Rupert can finesse an MBE out of this tour, he's all set to go back to the battalion as 2ic after which he should pick up his half Colonel. A couple of years as DS at Shriv followed by command would be nice. Fast track to Brigade command a distinct possibility, provided he doesn't let anyone else fuck it up for him. Does it matter that nobody likes him? Not really; they simply need to understand that it's a dog-eat-dog career and there are no prizes for second place.

SARAH SWIFT

Everyone's a bit scared of Sarah. Maybe it's her background as a Corporal in the RMP; maybe it's the fact that she's captain of Army Women's Triathlon; maybe she's just a bit fierce. Whatever: there is no question that if any glass ceilings appear, she's going to kick her way through them.

She's almost lost the accent now but she grew up in the Potteries where some of her friends were poor enough to live in real deprivation. Sarah's family were fine: Dad was a warehouse manager and Mum was an office manager in the NHS, but they never had a lot of money. Sarah joined the Army after A levels because she didn't want all the student debt from university. Basic was easy, phase 2 a doddle; and her ability to focus, combined with her steely determination to do well at everything, meant she was picked out as a potential officer before she was out of training. First posting was two years in Cyprus, including a six-monther in Basra, but by then things were done and dusted. With AOSB under her belt, she was off to Sandhurst.

Sandhurst was good. A commission in the AGC SPS and a first posting as a Det Commander in the Household Division was a good start.

The Army has a plan. They want Sarah to do an SO3 job in HQ 16 Air Assault, and they want her to pass P Company and do the Para Course. It's a nice idea and Sarah knows that, in ideal conditions, she could certainly get through on the same basis as any of the guys. The issue for her is that, as a 9 stone woman, the chances of picking up an injury are high. Sarah is challenging for a place in the national squad and 2012 is close enough to focus the mind.

The choice is to stick with the Army and see where it takes her – and there's no doubt she could do very, very well – or to leave and perhaps spend the next couple of years competing on the Triathlon circuit. Sarah's boyfriend Greg owns an outdoor pursuits centre in North Wales which takes underprivileged kids out into the mountains and the lakes, and he's offered Sarah a partnership in this and perhaps for the rest of her life as well. Decisions, decisions.

SOLDIERS

DAN STEELE

Nobody believes him, but Dan was actually born in London, at St George's Hospital in Tooting. According to his mum, she spent the minimum time possible in the grey, miserable city before taking him back to their cattle ranch in newly independent Zimbabwe. Dan's parents saw the writing on the wall and sold up in the early 1990s, moving to Cape Town, where they opened a building supplies business. They did fine in South Africa. Dan and his brother went to St John's College, but Dan spent more time playing rugby and chasing girls than he did studying, so the plan to go to a British university was a bit of a non-starter. He started a business degree in Cape Town but dropped out in the first year. Instead, he decided to have a go at joining the British Army. This was becoming a problem for South Africans thanks to the mercenary laws, but Dan had his British passport, so not a problem. Next stop AOSB at Westbury.

Uh-oh. Most of the others in Dan's syndicate at briefing were flabby, unfit Brits. Dan had been brought up in a world where you call a spade a spade (and sometimes worse) and didn't hesitate to tell them so. The result was a cat 4: fuck off, being an officer in the British Army is not for you.

Undeterred, Dan got himself a job as a barman in London and began the process of enlisting as a soldier in the Parachute Regiment. Fuck it, might as well join the best. A physically fit natural athlete, Dan was best Parachute Regiment recruit at Catterick and cruised P Company. If he hadn't been such a hard bastard, his cockiness might have earned him a few digs on the way. Dan got his first tape eighteen months after joining the battalion. He's due a second, but as a volunteer for SAS selection it's temporarily on hold. No one doubts he'll get through the walking but his temperament may count against him, particularly in the jungle, if he gets the wrong DS. Time will tell.

DAZ THE DINOSAUR

When Daz Crowe joined up in 1988, his dad had basically been unemployed for five years. As a result, home was not a happy place and young Darren was desperate to get out. With no work locally, the Army looked like the only option.

The recruiter steered Daz towards the Paras: he was an angry young man, but he was motivated too and nobody's fool. Depot Para in Aldershot was a tough school but it didn't break Daz. During the P Company milling, the DS had to pull him off his opponent and pin him down, to stop him lashing out at them too. Once in the battalion he was in his element.

There've been a couple of fuck ups along the way. Daz married Christine in Aldershot when he was 19 and she was 22. If he's honest, he did it to get out of the shithole block in Montgomery Lines. He can see now it was a mistake and that he was wrong to think he could carry on

living like a single bloke with a wife and – soon – a kid in tow. After 20 months he moved back into the block to get away from her moaning and the baby crying. He hasn't seen a lot of Craig while he's been growing up but he seems to have grown into a decent enough lad. Daz remarried four years ago, the widow of one of his mates who was killed in Afghan: this time it seems to be working. Daz took over the mortgage on the flat in Collie, and she hasn't got any kids, thank fuck.

Daz honestly thinks he doesn't mind if you're black, white, straight, gay or female if you can do your job; but if you can't, you've got no business in the Army and certainly not in the Reg. Here's the problem: 'they' just won't let you do your job any more. When Daz was a crow – and he heard all the fucking jokes back then, ta – if you fucked something up, your section commander, platoon sergeant or company sergeant major took you round the back of the company office and gave you a bit of a dig to let you know not to do it again. Nowadays, that's 'bullying' FFS!

Daz made it to WO2. Not bad. He thought about SAS selection at one stage but then thought, 'fuck it, at the end of the day most of them are just hats, anyway'. Now he's got a job lined up doing CP for one of the big PMCs operating in Iraq: good money, and mostly good blokes too. Eight weeks on, four weeks off: can't be bad.

SAMMI DENT

Sammi knew what a lesbian was when she joined up, but she had no idea she was one. It took four or five years after she joined, and several going-nowhere relationships, before she began to perceive that she was just much more into her girlfriends than she was into the blokes she'd been out with and, occasionally, slept with. It took a little while to come to terms with, but now she's comfortable. She's got a steady partner and they're looking into buying a flat together somewhere near ATR Winchester where they both work.

The trouble is that a lot of the blokes she works with seem to think that her lesbianism is a challenge to their masculinity. She thought they'd get over it, and to be fair most of them have, but there's a hard-core minority who still think it's funny to SMS pictures of their cocks to her, or email her links to porn sites. Some of the guys doing this are so stupid, ugly and unappealing that she wouldn't want to fuck them if she was a heterosexual nymphomaniac and they were the last men left alive on the planet. The really irritating thing is some of the seniors and officers seem to think it's funny too. The thing is, she knows that if she makes a complaint they'll close ranks and claim she's 'playing the sexism card' and everything she's done in her private life – and like everyone, she's made a few mistakes – will get dragged out into the open.

So she's going to keep her head down and put up with it. It is slowly changing for the better, but the Army's a conservative institution and change is always slow.

TECHNICAL TIM

Tim's parents really weren't too sure about him joining the Army. At his school in the East Midlands he was at or near the top in all the important subjects and Mum and Dad saw him staying local, combining college with an apprenticeship at one of the local engineering companies. There was good money to be made, and above all it was safe. In the end they only agreed to let him join up because Tim wanted to go into a technical trade. They signed the forms, and not long after his GCSEs Tim was at Harrogate as an apprentice in the Royal Signals, the first step on the path towards becoming a radio tech. It certainly wasn't an easy process, but Tim was more on top of it than most and by the time the trade was amalgamated with the radio relay techs and terminal equipment techs to form the systems engineer tech trade, Tim was cruising. A tour with 264 (SAS) Sigs Squadron and playing corps football didn't do any harm either, and Tim was an obvious candidate for selection to train as a Foreman of Signals.

Tim met and married Maureen during a Northern Ireland tour but they decided to buy a house in Hampshire in a nice, quiet, safe area, not far from Basingstoke, where Maureen can crack on with her nursing. Tim's twenty-two is up in eighteen months and while he's a dead cert for a commission, the fact is he'll get five times what he's earning now if he jumps across to the telecoms industry, so why on earth would he stay? He'll miss the banter and the organized sport, but he isn't going to miss having to explain the basics to clueless officers, or the general petty annoyances either. Tim's grateful for what the Army's given him, but he feels he's given a lot back too, and the deal's about even. Time to move on.

TOM BULLER

There was never any doubt which regiment Tom was going to join. In fact as far as he is concerned, there is only one regiment: the Grenadiers. Tom's father was a Grenadier and his father before him too. And his grandfather on his mother's side was RSM of the second battalion; she can still bull up a pair of toecaps almost as well as Tom can, and Tom was making his Spiderman bedspread up with hospital corners from the age of three.

Tom is at Sandhurst now: Company Sergeant Major in New College. Standards may be dropping in some other training establishments – Tom doesn't really care – but they aren't going to drop at the Royal Military Academy. The cadets in Tom's company are starched, pressed and polished within an inch of their lives.

And Tom isn't just about bullshit either. He knows that in less than a year a good few of these young gentlemen will be leading soldiers on operations in Afghanistan. Tom was Mentioned in Despatches in Iraq and lost part of a finger to an IED fragment in Helmand, so he can walk the walk and talk the talk. At a lean six foot four and with a voice like a megaphone, he can be terrifying on the drill square, but he's a good sport and very approachable socially, and the cadets look on him as a kind of god.

The whisper from Glasgow is that Tom will be going back to the battalion as RQMS and then back to Sandhurst as a College RSM, after which a commission is the odds-on bet. One up on Tom's dad, who only made it to Colour Sergeant.

Tom's son Martin isn't that keen on the Army. It isn't a big issue; he's looking at the Met Police, which is perfectly respectable. Strangely, daughter Lauren is quite keen. She's a county-level hockey player for her age group and a fanatical member of the CCF at her boarding school in Dorset. Tom has a sneaking suspicion that she might be commissioned at about the same time he is. It's just a shame it can't be in the Grenadiers.

THE ARMY AIR CORPS
Teeny-Weeny Airways; the Twenty-Minuters

Who are these sky gods in their butch powder-blue berets? The Army Air Corps, that's who. These modern-day successors to the Royal Flying Corps and the Glider Pilot Regiment suddenly started packing real heat in 2000 when they acquired – much to the annoyance of the RAF, who wanted it themselves – the Apache attack helicopter to supplement their hitherto somewhat flaccid collection of reconnaissance and utility aircraft. The Apache is a kick-ass machine, like a flying X-Box with real guns, missiles and rockets, originally envisaged as an aerial tankbuster but which has proved just as adept in kinetic counter-insurgency operations in Iraq and Afghanistan.

Unlike the RAF, where only officers are allowed to fly aircraft (although, to be fair, it is hard to tell officers and other ranks apart in the RAF), pilots in the Army Air Corps are Corporals and above. Officers command the units; they don't necessarily have to do the driving too.

In fact, if you join the AAC as a soldier (an 'Airtrooper'), you train initially

Hurrah for the Twenty-Minuters!

as a groundie, specializing in communications or various aviation support skills, and can then apply to be trained as aircrew as a doorgunner, systems operator or winchman – or, once you've got to substantive Lance Jack, as a pilot, provided you pass aircrew selection and flying grading. DE officers are all trained as pilots, which adds an extra layer of selection to the process, but unlike the RAF they are primarily roled as officers – commanding, leading and managing men and units. The real specialist flyers in the AAC tend to be senior NCOs, Warrant Officers and LE officers.

Corporals and above can also volunteer to do a flying tour from elsewhere in the Army. You need the eyesight of a particularly sharp-eyed hawk, pass aircrew selection and flying grading, as well as the pilots course which is hard work, but if you succeed you get to hob-nob with the royal family and all sorts of other undesirables.

The main effort of the AAC is located with 16 Air Assault Brigade, which has three aviation regiments (Apache/Lynx), but there are additional AAC units scattered about, supporting British Army activity in various exotic locations. The AAC regiments are:

1 **Regiment, AAC – Gutersloh**, Germany. Lynx.
2 **(Training) Regiment, AAC** – Middle Wallop. Trains aircrew on Apache, Lynx, Gazelle.
3 **Regiment, AAC – Wattisham**. Apache and Lynx, part of 16 Air Assault Brigade.
4 **Regiment, AAC – Wattisham**. Apache and Lynx, part of 16 Air Assault Brigade.
5 **Regiment, AAC – Aldergrove**, Northern Ireland. Gazelle.
6 **(Volunteer) Regiment, AAC** – TA.
9 **Regiment, AAC** – Dishforth. Apache and Lynx, part of 16 Air Assault Brigade.

Independent AAC sub-units:

7 **Flight AAC – Brunei.**
8 **Flight AAC – Hereford**, in support of 22 SAS.
25 **Flight AAC – Belize.**
29 **(BATUS) Flight AAC – Suffield**, Canada.
657 **Squadron – RAF Odiham**, SF support.

[LIVING THE ARMY LIFE] CHICKEN SUPREME

One of the four blessed menus of tinned rations, Chicken Supreme was chicken curry without the curry. A useful 'tabula rasa' for the compo gourmets out there which could be improved beyond all recognition by the addition of freshly fried onions, chilli peppers, a swirl of double cream and a hefty dose of freshly ground black pepper. But, frankly, why would you bother?

Also known, to those with some knowledge of anatomy and those foolish enough to look too closely (and also, obviously, to those dismal capitalists or wageslaves respectively who took the taxpayers' money to fabricate this muck and subsequently deem it fit to feed the forces), as 'Major Vessels in Body Fluid Sauce'.

APACHE SPECIFICATION	
Length:	14.97m
Rotorspan:	5.23m
Height:	4.95m
MTOW:	22,282lb
Maximum speed:	162mph
Maximum range:	1,180 miles
Service ceiling:	9,470ft
Climb rate:	2,415ft/min
Armament:	1 × 30mm cannon
Mission Specific Armament:	16 × AGM-114 Hellfire anti-tank missiles 4 × Hydra-70 2.75in 7/14-Shot rocket pods 4 × Hydra-70 2.75in 14-Shot rocket pods 18 × Stinger air-to-air missiles 2 × AIM-9 Sidewinder missiles 2 × Sidearm ARM (Anti-Radiation) missiles

Apache

The WAH-64D used by the Army Air Corps is a significant and ballsy piece of kit with the capability to influence events on both low- and high-intensity battlefields decisively. Easily capable of defeating any battlefield AFV, it is also rugged enough to withstand punishment that would reduce most helicopters to tangled scrap. Sadly, its reputation for invincibility was slightly dented when a couple of Iraqi militiamen armed with bolt-action rifles brought one down during the early stages of the invasion of Iraq. Even so, it is a mighty piece of kit.

Gazelle

Also known as the Screaming Chicken Leg, the Gayzelle, Battle Sperm and the Floppy. Lightweight Anglo-French reconnaissance and liaison helicopter with all the survivability of a chocolate teapot. Cruises at 120 knots, so officers can work out how long to get somewhere (clue: two nautical miles a minute). Features an enclosed tail rotor called a 'fenestron'. Has the capacity to carry three passengers in addition to the pilot, but only if they weigh no more than a can of Diet Coke, otherwise the thing will never get off the ground. They can be fitted with several external accessories, none of which are likely to convince potential passengers of the safety record of these helicopters. The gearbox never decapitates people on crashing, and no one (while on groundcrew duty in Northern Ireland) ever performed the feat called 'Blade Running' – that is, no one ever climbed on top of the rotor disk and ran down the blades, leaping off the end before the springyness brought it back up to hit you in the back. No one ever lost big flaps of skin from their backs as the trim on the end gouged holes out of you. It simply never happened.

The Gazelle has been compared to shagging a fat chick and riding a scooter: both can be fun but you wouldn't want your mates to see you doing it.

Originally in tri-service use, but now only in the Army Air Corps. The only three gayer helicopters are the Skeeter, the Squirrel and – the wettest, most pouffiest of all things ever flown – the Sioux. There are those who would contest that the Agusta 109 is also gay, but it's actually quite nails. It must be: the SAS use them.

HELICOPTERS
THE HARDWARE → [AVIATION]

LYNX SPECIFICATION	
Crew:	3
Capacity:	Up to ten passengers
Maximum speed:	324 kmh
Range:	528 km

Lynx

The Lynx is the finest anti-submarine helicopter ever operated by the British Army. Ever. The elongated nose characteristic of the type is widely believed by those not in receipt of flying pay to be an extension to accommodate the pilot's wallet. Housed in the back amid porn and blagged choccie bars you will often find the hulking, gurgling form of a door gunner.

Variants

There are three main variants still in UK service.

Lynx AH Mk7: Mostly recycled AH1 airframes with a new gearbox which could manage the power output from slightly less wheezy engines, and more butt-strapping down the tailboom. They were originally procured as an anti-tank aircraft equipped with eight TOW missiles although this system went out of service in 68 BC. The aircraft will continue to soldier on in the utility role until the arrival of BLUH (in service date, 2042; current fleet due to fall out of the sky, 2012). Instantly recognizable by the fact that it has skids and 200 litres of oil over every battered panel. The engines never need an oil-change: being mounted at six degrees from the horizontal, all the oil is automatically dumped on shutdown. Room in the back for two camp-beds. In theory a twin-engined aircraft, it rarely lands in such a condition. Handles like a Ferrari and by coincidence is as reliable and as costly to run.

Lynx Mk 9: Bought in the late eighties/early nineties to provide the Army with a utility aircraft capable of carrying more than a small map (see Gazelle). Main tasking has always been the delivery of soup to the troops, hence the nickname of Soup Dragons.

THE HARDWARE → [AVIATION]

Also known as the Wheelybin. Used to have a very vulnerable nose oleo that made a really scary noise when it broke. Mainwheel oleos are allegedly sourced from a big bin of Whirlwind bits.

Lynx Mk 8: Operated by the Royal Navy, carries Stingray torpedoes, Sea Skua anti-ship missiles, GPMG, .50-cal machine gun and depth charges, and therefore not worthy of further comment.

Operational Service
The Lynx Mk 7 saw action during Operation Granby when a particularly aggressive cardboard box was heavily disguised as a cardboard box and was therefore engaged by a certain RCT Captain, thus beginning the battle of Box Hill. The Lynx has also been serving in Northern Ireland since the late 1970s.

Wisdom
Old Lynx pilot's proverb: 'If something hasn't broken/fallen off/caught fire/exploded/failed/destroyed itself into oblivion/eaten itself/generally stopped functioning, it's either just about to or it's sat in the hangar.'

COMBAT SUPPORT ARMS

Combat Support Arms provide direct support to the fighting troops in the front line.

The Royal Artillery: where a pat on the back is only ever a recce.

THE ROYAL REGIMENT OF ARTILLERY

The Gunners (traditional); the Dropshorts

The corps that's first among the ladies, and amazin' first in war! 'Artillery, the essence of military power' – so said Stalin. Napoleon put it differently: 'It is with the guns,' he said, 'that war is made.'

But the fact is that if you get more than three or four Gunner officers together at any one time, there'll be blood on the carpet as they claw, scratch and bite at each other to improve their promotion chances. Paradoxically, Gunners also have a widespread and mostly deserved reputation throughout the Army for being penis-mutilatingly boring. Go figure.

The regiment is an organization that strikes fear into every heart, friend and enemy alike. The bad guys get large chunks of metal raining down on them from miles away, but let's face it, dropping a few short is not entirely unknown to the brave lads and lasses of the Royal Artillery. Even more frightening is the visible aura of tedium that accompanies Gunner officers everywhere. Once they hit the rank of Major they are injected with a special hormone that turns them into doctrine-spouting, jargon-yammering bores. It can only have been a Gunner who invented the meaningless new buzzword 'Non-Kinetic Strike', or started all that shit about referring to artillery support as 'Fires'.

As they spent much of their time with bits of equipment that made startlingly loud noises, Gunners of the past (not in these health-and-safety-conscious days, no siree) were apt to suffer hearing damage, a condition known as 'Gunner Ear'. This may explain why Gunners never actually listen to anything you tell them.

The Gunners have three main roles:

1 Close support field artillery with the AS90 self-propelled 155mm gun, the 105mm light gun and Multiple Launch Rocket Systems.

2 Air Defence ('Cloudpunchers').

3 Surveillance and Target Acquisition (STA) using UAVs, weapon-locating radars, sound ranging and STA patrols.

There are a range of different careers available to soldiers but what they have in common is that Phase 2 training takes place in Larkhill, a garrison that makes nearby Bulford and Tidworth seem FOO fighters. exotically attractive. Officers tend to get shuttled around between the close support and air defence roles to some extent, but have an early advantage in the Army in that they get to see the all-arms concept at work from quite an early stage. In addition to being organized functionally, the Gunners are also divided between the 'Royal Artillery' and the 'Royal Horse Artillery'. Officers in the RHA try to give the impression that they are a tad grander and more elitist than their field artillery counterparts – a bit of the cavalry/infantry vibe going on – but the division is now essentially meaningless, with the exception of 7 RHA, the airborne artillery regiment, which requires officers and soldiers to have passed P Company, thus constituting a form of elitism (but which is counterbalanced by 29 Commando Regiment Royal Artillery anyway).

The major units of the Gunners are:

AS90-equipped Field Regiments
1st Regiment, the Royal Horse Artillery (1 RHA) –
Assaye Barracks, Tidworth.
3rd Regiment, the Royal Horse Artillery, 'The Liverpool
and Manchester Gunners' (3 RHA) – Caen Barracks, Hohne.

[LIVING THE ARMY LIFE] CHOGIE WALLAHS

Chogie Wallahs (or Char Wallahs) are one of the last survivals in British military tradition from our imperial past in India. Muslim traders, they supplied everything a soldier might need on operations. They set up their shops in British Army bases across the globe and doled out laundry, egg banjos, cheeseburgers, flasks of coffee, t-shirts, beer, pornographic magazines and everything else you could possibly think of, 7 days a week, 24 hours a day. If they didn't have it in the shop, they'd get it for you in 24 hours, or possibly 48 if it was the Ark of the Covenant, a 1933 penny or a solid gold SA-80.

This can-do attitude got up the noses of the can't-do NAAFI hierarchy and the Chogies have been slowly expelled from British bases. Sadly, NAAFI haven't tried to replicate the services the Chogies offered: they just didn't like the competition.

The IRA murdered two of these men. Outside their own families they won't be remembered by anyone much, so let's do it here:

Noor Baz Khan, murdered on 26 May 1973 in Londonderry

Mohammed Abdul Khan, murdered on 22 April 1974 at Ford's Cross

4th Regiment, Royal Artillery, 'The North East Gunners' (4 Regt RA) – Alanbrooke Barracks, Topcliffe.

19th Regiment, Royal Artillery, 'The Highland Gunners' (9 Regt RA) – Bhurtpore Barracks, Tidworth.

26th Regiment, Royal Artillery, 'The West Midland Gunners' (26 Regt RA) – Mansergh Barracks, Gutersloh.

MLRS-equipped Field Regiments

39th Regiment, Royal Artillery (39 Regt RA) – Albemarle Barracks, Ouston.

Air Defence Regiments

12th Regiment, Royal Artillery, 'The Lancashire and Cumbrian Gunners' (12 Regt RA), equipped with HVM and UAV – Baker Barracks, Thorney Island.

16th Regiment, Royal Artillery, 'The London and Kent Gunners' (16 Regt RA), equipped with RAPIER – St George's Barracks, North Luffenham.

47th Regiment, Royal Artillery, 'The Hampshire and Sussex Gunners' (47 Regt RA), equipped with HVM – Baker Barracks, Thorney Island.

Surveillance and Target Acquisition Regiments

5th Regiment, Royal Artillery, 'The North, East & West Yorkshire Gunners' (5 Regt RA) – Marne Barracks, Catterick.

32nd Regiment, Royal Artillery (32 Regt RA) – Roberts Barracks, Larkhill.

Light Gun-equipped Field Regiments

7th (Parachute) Regiment, the Royal Horse Artillery, 'The Airborne Gunners' (7 (Para) RHA) – Kirkee Barracks, Colchester.

29th Commando Regiment, Royal Artillery, 'The Commando Gunners' (29 Cdo Regt RA) – Royal Citadel, Plymouth.

7 (Sphinx) Commando Battery RA – RM Condor, Arbroath

148 (Meiktila) Commando Forward Observation Battery RA – RM Poole.

40th Regiment, Royal Artillery, 'The Lowland Gunners' (40 Regt RA) – Lisburn.

The TA Regiments

100th (Yeomanry) Regiment, Royal Artillery (Volunteers) – 100 Regt RA(V), equipped with Light Gun.

101st (Northumbrian) Regiment, Royal Artillery (Volunteers) – 101 Regt RA(V), equipped with MLRS.

103rd (Lancashire Artillery Volunteers) Regiment, Royal Artillery (Volunteers) – 103 Regt RA(V), equipped with Light Gun.

104th Regiment, Royal Artillery (Volunteers) – 104 Regt RA(V), equipped with HVM.

105th (Scottish & Ulster) Regiment, Royal Artillery (Volunteers) – 105 Regt RA(V), equipped with Light Gun.

106th (Yeomanry) Regiment, Royal Artillery (Volunteers) – 106 Regt RA(V), equipped with HVM and RAPIER.

. . . And Last But Not Least

The Honourable Artillery Company. Not actually part of the Royal Regiment of Artillery, the HAC is a hybrid TA STA/artillery/ceremonial regiment/private club with links to the Royal Artillery, Foot Guards and Special Forces.

AS90 SPECIFICATION	
Crew:	5
Length:	9.07m
Height to turret roof:	2.49m
Width:	3.5m
Ground clearance:	0.41m
Main armament:	1 × L31 39-calibre 155mm gun
Ammunition carried:	48 × 155mm rounds
Secondary armament:	1 × 7.62 GPMG on turret for air defence
Engine:	Cummins VTA903T turbocharged V8 660bhp diesel

AS90

Ninety-nine times out of a hundred when you see an AS90 in the media it will be described as a tank. It isn't. It's a self-propelled artillery piece. What's the difference? A tank is a highly mobile, well-protected armoured fighting vehicle with a main armament designed to take out other AFVs at a maximum range of around two miles. A self-propelled gun like the AS90 is actually relatively lightly protected (its armour is proof against small arms and fragmentation only) and the main armament is designed to lob high-explosive artillery shells on to precision targets at ranges of 30km or so with standard ammunition and up to 60–80km with extended-range ammunition. So there.

Interestingly, many British self-propelled artillery systems since WW2 have had ecclesiastical names (Abbot, Priest and so on). The AS90 took so long and cost so much money to get into service that it has been unofficially named 'the Choirboy', as it spent twelve years being buggered by Vickers.

ARTILLERY

GMLRS SPECIFICATION	
Crew:	3
Rate of fire:	12 rockets per minute
Re-load time:	3-4 minutes
Range:	Up to 70 km

GMLRS

When you absolutely really and truly want to fuck up someone's day, there are a couple of ways the Royal Artillery can help you. Firstly, they can invite them to a social function in their Officers' Mess. If that doesn't work, there's always GMLRS as a fall-back.

Described by its users as the 'Grid Square Removal Service', GMLRS is a rocket system capable of launching guided munitions out beyond 70km (that's more than 40 miles to you diehard imperialists) with the capability of literally blanketing a square kilometre with nasty pointy sharp stuff whanging around at supersonic velocities. Many's the Taliban, sitting happily in a trench dreaming up more devilry, who has found himself being painfully eviscerated by a Gunner who was probably already stirring the sugar into his brew by the time his munitions arrived on target. It's worth a thought.

ARTILLERY

Light Gun

A 105mm light towed field gun used by the Airborne and Commando Batteries of the Royal Artillery, and occasionally by other batteries when operating in support of light role forces. The LG can lob a shell containing just under 3kg of high explosive to a range of 17,200 metres at a rate of six to eight rounds per minute – quite enough to fuck someone's day up. A less powerful version, the L119, is in use with the US Marine Corps.

Rapier

Rapier is a point air defence missile system which, in one form or another, has been in service with the Royal Artillery since 1971. It was originally developed as an optically guided system that used radar to acquire a target aircraft and an optical sight for the operator to guide the missile to the target. Over the course of development up to the current Field Standard C the process has now been fully automated, with the missile guided by radar. Range is from 400m to 6.8km.

ARTILLERY

STARSTREAK HVM SPECIFICATION	
Vehicle:	CVRT Stormer
Guidance :	SACLOS laser guidance system
Range:	0.3 – 7km
Warhead:	3 explosive darts
Velocity:	Mach 3.5

Starstreak HVM

Starstreak HVM is a lightweight anti-aircraft missile system introduced in 1997 to complement the Rapier system and supersede the Javelin system (which had itself superseded the crappy Blowpipe system). It's in service with the Air Defence 'Cloudpunchers' of the Royal Artillery and can be launched from the CVR(T) Stormer variant, or from a portable launcher module.

It works through optical tracking and laser guidance. The operator tracks the target through the stabilized optical site while the guidance unit computes a solution; when this is done the missile is launched and it heads towards the target at Mach 3.5. When the second-stage rocket has burned out, three sub-munitions deploy and zip towards the target in formation, thus increasing the chance of a hit. The sub-munitions work on a contact fuze designed to allow the munition to penetrate the target aircraft before setting off an explosive charge. There is no proximity fuze so the munitions do need to score a direct hit. The effective range is from 300m out to 7km.

THE CORPS OF ROYAL ENGINEERS
The Sappers (traditional); the Wedge; the Wedgeheads

The Sappers are truly the Army's 'jacks of all trades', turning their hands to all kinds of tasks from building bridges, laying minefields and bomb disposal all the way through to making maps. By and large they're nice enough blokes too, although you do seem to find quite a few officers and seniors with the wild-eyed look about them of crusading Victorian missionaries. Never mind: among their finer qualities is their unrivalled ability to conjure up a functioning bar out of more or less nothing. At Basra Airport in 2003, it was the Wedge who got the first bar up and running as the beer began to flow in from Um Qasr, and while in theory it was restricted to Sappers and their guests only, it turned out that they'd invited everyone in the division. Way to go Sappers!

Having a huge range of roles means that the lads and lasses in the Wedge are a mixed bunch, ranging from dull-eyed diggers of holes and shovellers of shit to highly technically qualified geo-techs and surveyors. Officers usually, but not always, have degrees in civil engineering and related disciplines. What they have in common is an air of practicality: they always seem to get things done when you need it.

Sapper tasks are broadly defined as mobility (enabling us to move around the battlespace), counter-mobility (preventing the enemy from doing so) and survivability (making sure that we are protected). This leads to specific roles for the Royal Engineers:

'Maybe we could build a bar out of mealie bags, Mr Bromhead.'

Close Support. Working in the combat zone at brigade and battlegroup level. Close support units are equipped and organized to meet the role of the formations they support but will usually consist of a mix of soft-skin and armoured vehicles including specialist engineer equipment.

General Support. Working out of contact providing specialist support for close support units as well as close support to the lines of communication.

Air Support. Working for the RAF building runways and other facilities that they require.

Explosive Ordnance Disposal. Provision of support in UK and on operations overseas. Traditionally, Sappers dug up and destroyed enemy ordnance like unexploded bombs while the Ammo Techs and ATOs of the RLC (and previously RAOC) dealt with terrorist IEDs. The tempo of operations in Afghanistan particularly means that Sapper EOD teams are now conducting 'render safe' procedures on IEDs as well.

Geographic. Providing mapping and geospatial support across defence.

Infrastructure Engineering. Designing and supervising the construction of all manner of very complicated things that the rest of their corps would not understand. In this role Sappers are intimately connected with the major reconstruction projects in Iraq, Afghanistan and elsewhere.

Major units of the Sappers are:

- 21 **Engineer Regiment** – Close Support – Ripon
- 22 **Engineer Regiment** – Close Support – Tidworth
- 23 **Engineer Regiment (Air Assault)**, part of 16 Air Assault Brigade
- 24 **Commando Engineer Regiment**, attached to 3 Commando Brigade, Royal Marines – Chivenor
- 25 **Engineer Regiment** – Air Support – Waterbeach
- 26 **Engineer Regiment** – Close Support – Tidworth
- 28 **Engineer Regiment** – General Support – Hameln (Germany)
- 32 **Engineer Regiment** – Close Support – Hohne (Germany)
- 33 **Engineer Regiment** – Explosive Ordnance Disposal and Advanced Search – Wimbish
- 35 **Engineer Regiment** – Close Support – Paderborn (Germany)
- 36 **Engineer Regiment** – General Support – Maidstone (36 Engr Regt includes the two squadrons of Queen's Gurkha Engineers)

ENGINEERS

TITAN SPECIFICATION	
Function:	Carries BR-90 Close Support Bridges: No. 10 (length 26m, span 21–24.5m), No. 11 (length 16m, span 14.5m), and No. 12 (length 13.5m, span 12m)
Crew:	3
Weight:	62,500kg
Maximum road speed:	59km/h
Road range:	450km
Armament:	stowage for crewman-portable light anti-tank weapons, fitted with NBC protection system
Engine:	Perkins CV12 diesel engine, David Brown TN54 enhanced low-loss gearbox and the OMANI cooling group. Auxiliary Power Unit (APU) is also fitted.
Engine power:	1,200bhp

Titan

Titan is the relatively new armoured bridge-laying system based on the chassis of the Challenger 2 and issued to Royal Engineers armoured close support regiments.

TROJAN SPECIFICATION	
Crew:	3
Weight:	62,500kg
Maximum road speed:	59km/h
Road range:	450km
Armament:	1 × 7.62mm machine gun; stowage for crewman-portable light anti-tank weapons, fitted with NBC protection system
Engine:	Perkins CV12 diesel engine, David Brown TN54 enhanced low-loss gearbox and the OMANI cooling group. Auxiliary Power Unit (APU) is also fitted.
Engine power:	1,200 bhp

Trojan

Not in fact an extra-durable condom for use by gay men but the latest successor to the venerable AVRE (in the original Churchill, Centurion and Chieftain) and the Combat Engineer Tractor. Like the Titan, Trojan is based on the Challenger 2 chassis and power train and offers various capabilities, including mine-laying, using fascines for obstacle crossing, mine-ploughing, bulldozing and excavation.

38 Engineer Regiment – Close Support – Antrim, NI
39 Engineer Regiment – Air Support – Waterbeach
42 Engineer Regiment (Geographic) – Hermitage
62 Cyprus Support Squadron Royal Engineers – Dhekelia, Cyprus

TA

Royal Monmouthshire Royal Engineers (Militia)
100 Field Squadron – Cwmbran/Bristol/Cardiff
101 Headquarters Troop – Monmouth
108 (Welsh) Field Squadron – Swansea/Gorseinion
225 Field Squadron – Birmingham
The Jersey Field Squadron – St Helier
71 Engineer Regiment (Volunteers) (Air Support)
102 (Clyde) Field Squadron (Air Support) – Paisley/ Barnsford Bridge
124 Field Squadron – Cumbernauld
236 Field Squadron – Elgin
Headquarters Troop – RAF Leuchars
10 Orkney Field Troop – Orkney Islands
72 Engineer Regiment (Volunteers) Close Support
103 (Tyne Electrical Engineers) Field Squadron (Air Support) – Newcastle/Sunderland
106 (West Riding) Field Squadron – Sheffield/Bradford
299 Para Field Squadron – Wakefield/Hull/Gateshead
73 Engineer Regiment (Volunteers) (Air Support)
129 Headquarters and Support Squadron – Nottingham
350 Field Squadron (Air Support) – Nottingham
575 (Sherwood Foresters) Field Squadron (Air Support) – Chesterfield
75 Engineer Regiment (Volunteers) (Field)
107 (Lancashire and Cheshire) Field Squadron – Birkenhead/St Helens
125 (Staffordshire) Field Support Squadron – Stoke-on-Trent
143 Plant Squadron – Walsall
201 Headquarters Squadron – Manchester
101 Engineer Regiment (EOD) (V)
217 (London) Field Squadron (EOD) – Holloway
221 Field Squadron (EOD) – Rochester/Catford
579 Field Squadron (EOD) – Tunbridge Wells

131 Independent Commando Squadron Royal Engineers (Volunteers) – London/Bath/Plymouth/Birmingham, part of 24 Commando Regiment RE

135 Independent Geographic Squadron Royal Engineers (Volunteers) – Ewell

591 Independent Field Squadron Royal Engineers – Bangor, County Down

THE CORPS OF ROYAL SIGNALS

The Scaleybacks; the Bleeps; Interflora

The Royal Signals are the Army's providers of communications and IT support. They do this directly at formation level and above, and indirectly below this level by providing training and support to units. The corps' motto is *Certa Cito*, meaning 'Swift and Sure', but I suspect that if the rest of the Army were to be asked, it would be something like 'Boring but Important'.

The modern British Army functions on communications and information, and someone has to provide the infrastructure for it – as long as it isn't me that gets jiffed to do it, I'll survive. The consequence of this role is that the Royal Signals are everywhere the Army is, and sometimes in large numbers. If you're deployed with the British Army anywhere in the world, you're never more than a few feet away from a member of the Royal Signals – they're a bit like rats or cockroaches! Easy as it is to take the piss, without them the whole shooting match would fall apart pretty quickly.

Royal Signals partial privatisation: now it can be told.

In addition to comms and IT, the Royal Signals also have a responsibility for electronic warfare – jamming, interception and direction finding – which is done in conjunction with the Intelligence Corps.

How It All Works

The mainstream role of the Royal Signals is providing communications and IT support for operational headquarters. Thus, each deployable Divisional Headquarters has a Signals Regiment associated with it and each deployable Brigade Headquarters has a Signals Squadron; in fact, most personnel who work in the HQs – the Commander, staff officers, clerks and so on – are on the posted strength of the Signals Regiment or Squadron for administrative purposes. These are formed into sub-units so that when the headquarters is in the field they can support the 'Main' headquarters, an alternate or 'step-up' headquarters, the Brigade or Divisional Support Group (the logistics headquarters) and the Brigade or

Divisional Commander's tactical headquarters.

In practice, what this means is that together with the comms systems – radios and data through Bowman and other systems, 'trunk' communications through Ptarmigan (still! . . . the last coal-fired comms system in NATO and always good for a larf when it repeatedly drops out during the Divisional Commander's co-ord conference because a mouse has nibbled through the Black Nasty holding it all together) – liaison teams, dispatch riders, rebroadcast detachments and so on, the Scaleys are also responsible for all the life support and protection. Thus, it isn't just boring old radios, no siree! At the same time that the more technically minded bleeps are revving up the comms, others are putting up the BFOTs (big fuck-off tents), putting out wire, digging trenches and stagging on; and yet more are cooking the scoff, sorting out where everyone is going to sleep and digging latrines (or at least siting the 'Turdises', or Portaloos).

In addition to their role with formation headquarters, Royal Signals also provide specialist communications support for Special Forces through 18 (UKSF) Signal Regiment which provides regular squadrons to support 22 SAS, SBS, SRR and SFSG, together with a TA squadron to support 21 and 23 SAS. Operational members of these squadrons all go through specialized selection and training procedures to ensure their fitness for role. Oddly enough, at the old recruiting days they held at Sandhurst the Royal Signals stand would be almost entirely manned by hard-faced men in sandy, maroon and green berets.

National Communications

2 Signal Brigade was formed to provide information and communications systems support to the Army and government in times of crisis. With its headquarters based in Corsham, Wiltshire, 2 (National Communications) Signal Brigade's units are located throughout the UK from Elgin in the north to Eastbourne on the south coast.

The brigade provides vital communications in times of crisis using its regular and TA regiments as its backbone. In recent years TA members of the brigade have been involved in providing communications systems to support the Army's Green Goddesses during the firefighters' disputes, the Gleneagles G8 conference, and the Commonwealth Games.

After an MoD review of the future of GMW (Government Machinery in War), 2 Brigade's tasking became obsolete. The government decided that a nuclear strike/accident was not likely enough to warrant funding of units committed to this mission. After some slick manoeuvres by the (then) Brigade Command, the brigade (and all its regiments) were saved and re-roled for UK operations providing information communications systems support to military personnel/units on MACA tasks. A further review of 2 Signal Brigade's role in April 2009 saw it downsized to one regular and five TA regiments.

The brigade maintains communications elements permanently on twelve hours' notice to move, including TA personnel. The TA units are the component for delivering communications capability rather than a general reserve like the remainder of the TA. The brigade effectively employs 80 per cent of TA Royal Signals personnel.

Electronic Warfare

Responsible for intercepting, direction finding and jamming the enemy's communications, 14 Signals Regiment has come to rest at Brawdy in South Wales, after interim stops at Hullavington and Osnabruck, en route from the original locations at Scheuen, Wesendorf, Langeleben and Taunton Barracks (Celle) in Germany. Originally formed from a number of troop- and squadron-sized units (notably 225, 226 Signal Squadron) in 1976, the regiment operated in support of 1 (BR) Corps throughout the 1980s until the abrupt demise of the communist threat, at which point the question 'Well, what's it for?' raised its head. This was obviously the wrong question if the answer was 'Working four-day weeks pointlessly fucking around in Brawdy when not on operations.'

The regiment is characterized by a particularly large concentration of attached arms, notably from the Intelligence Corps, which brings a touch of class to what would otherwise be an odd unit full of Royal Signals 'Regimental Duty' types. Join this unit as a Specialist Operator and you will find yourself overseas at least six months of the year. So don't get married.

This unit is also the home of the Light Electronic Warfare Unit. These geezers are all Para trained etc. and are deployed on a regular basis to provide tactical intelligence to the front-line combat units. Grrr!

Appropriately enough, the regiment, based as it is closer to Dublin than London, also contains one of the largest concentrations of foreign-language linguists in the Army. No doubt this is useful in the fleshpots of Haverfordwest. In 1980 the unit distinguished itself by sending a linguist who was fluent in Mandarin and Cantonese to NI when he'd requested a posting to Hong Kong.

Who Joins?

The Royal Signals recruits pretty much across the gamut, from your basic honest grunt (or bleep) up to the kind of person who makes the average officer look comically ill-educated. There are members of the Royal Signals who will spend their careers digging holes, stagging on and then supervising others who are digging holes and stagging on, and then there are non-commissioned members of the Royal Signals who cop a BSc degree as part of their training. Follow the 'regimental' route and you get to be a gruff RSM or SSM, but the smart boys and girls in the Scaleys wind up as Yeoman of Signals (Yoz), Foreman of Signals (Foz), Supervisor Radio or the new super swanky 'Supervisor Information Systems'. With these guys, you get the strange feeling that you're talking to a McKinsey management consultant who is unaccountably wearing a camouflaged uniform.

THE INTELLIGENCE CORPS
Green Slime; Snot Hats; Spooks; Noddy's Commandos

Historically, service in the Intelligence Corps was seen as a slightly geeky option which attracted bright and occasionally devious soldiers, and unambitious, asthmatic, socially awkward, bespectacled officers who couldn't realistically expect to get past the rank of Major. Career management for both officers and soldiers was dubious and the Int Corps was no more part of the mainstream Army than the Veterinary Corps.

All that has changed over the last twenty-five years. The campaign in Northern Ireland, the end of the Cold War and the subsequent conflicts in the Balkans, as well as the various operations in the Middle East, have demonstrated the importance of effective intelligence, and the Int Corps has raised its game to meet this need. The corps has, in recent years, produced

How the Intelligence Corps imagine themselves.

a crop of respected generals and has firmly established itself as a mainstream, indispensable branch of the Army with a bright future.

From the career point of view, Intelligence Corps soldiers are promoted to Lance Corporal as soon as they finish their training and promotion is generally relatively rapid and well managed thereafter. A substantial number of Int Corps Warrant Officers receive LE commissions into the corps, while junior NCOs are regularly commissioned as DE officers into the corps as well as other arms and services. The nature of their task means that most Int Corps 'operators' will come into contact with exotic organizations like MI5, MI6, GCHQ and Special Forces during their careers, and they get to take part in high-level operational planning, which can be very rewarding from a professional point of view. So, competition for a commission in the Int Corps is fierce and its officers are now in the mainstream with the other combat and combat support arms, competing with them for senior appointments on a level playing field.

If you knew how this had been stirred, would you drink it?

On the other hand, despite their specialized role, day-to-day activity for most members of the corps is not that different to other personnel who work in and around the military staff branches. They will spend just as much time making brews, washing down Land Rovers, putting up 12×12 tents, gluing maps together and stirring staff officers' coffee with their knobs as anyone else working in a headquarters, and operational deployments are regular and frequent.

The role of the corps is to provide the Army with intelligence and security. There are two main career paths in the Int Corps for the young Padawan learner to follow.

The Light Side

Officially 'Operator Military Intelligence', this is the generalists stream in the Int Corps. OPMIs are normally to be found in MI battalions, companies and sections stationed around the UK and Germany where they provide intelligence and security support to both operational and regional formations. Does this make them into James Bond? Nope: for the most part the job consists of collating and analysing information collected by a wide range of sources, and then briefing this to operational commanders and staff. Alternatively, for security sections, the job consists of making sure that personnel, sensitive information and equipment are secure – and investigating what has gone wrong when it all goes missing.

'Luke, I am your first reporting officer...'

Outside the MI battalions, Intelligence Corps lightsiders are also employed providing support for customers including the Ministry of Defence, Special Forces and some diplomatic posts. Imagery analysts are also technically lightsiders, although in many ways what they do bears a much closer resemblance to work on . . .

The Dark Side

This is all about intercepting and analysing enemy communications, and this is the main area in which the Intelligence Corps – in conjunction with GCHQ, the Royal Signals and various others – is actually collecting intelligence. It's very sensitive stuff, and the nickname 'darksiders' comes from the fact that, for security reasons, very few of the buildings they work in operationally have any windows. Many 'darksiders' receive language training to a very high level as part of their trade training and this often means they will receive some postings to the 'light side' in liaison, interrogation and agent handling roles, among others. This doesn't mean darksiders don't get out in the field: a lot of tactical electronic warfare takes place right in the front line of operations. Lance Corporal Jabron Hashmi, the first British Muslim soldier killed in Afghanistan, was an Int Corps darksider operating in the heart of Helmand province.

Sneaky Stuff

For the most part, the role of the Int Corps is to analyse and collate information from other sources and convert it into intelligence, but members of the corps can get their hands dirty as collectors of Humint – intelligence gathered from human sources through interrogation, debriefing and the recruiting and running of agents. However, it's worth noting that although largely controlled by the Intelligence Corps this isn't an exclusively Int Corps activity: officers and soldiers, male and female, can volunteer for it from all parts of the Army and Royal Marines.

Casual Labour

The TA Int Corps is possibly better integrated with the regulars than any other unit. Consequently, members display all of the bizarre personality traits expected from someone with the cap-badge.

TA soldiers have been deploying on operations since . . . well, for ever. From Corporate to Granby, the Balkans to Veritas and all flavours of Telic and Herrick, the TA have been a part of the landscape in int cells all over the globe. Mobilization does however adversely affect the TA soldier's career as they miss out on promotion courses and face-time with the hierarchy while doing a useful job.

The majority of TA soldiers are to be found in 3(V) MI Bn. Run out of a swirling admin vortex masquerading as a TA centre in central London, they have TACs all over the country. The newly formed 5 (V) MI Bn has its headquarters in the Midlands.

Joining

If you want to join the Int Corps as a soldier, you need to achieve a high score in the initial BARB test at the Army Careers Information Office, and you need at least five GCSEs at grade C or above; many Int Corps soldiers also have A levels, and a good few join with degrees (the Int Corps is often a fall-back for individuals who fail officer selection).

If you intend to try for a commission the requirements are the same as for the rest of the Army (180 UCAS points), but the reality is that you will be competing for a limited number of places with people with top degrees from elite universities. It certainly isn't impossible for a non-graduate to be commissioned in the corps, but they'd have to bring something special to the table.

[LIVING THE ARMY LIFE] EGG BANJO

Food of the gods. An egg banjo consists of:
- two slices of white bread (dirty fingerprints are desirable but not obligatory);
- one greasy fried egg;
- butter or margarine;
- either red sauce or brown sauce.

It may additionally contain bacon or sausage, but nothing else. Any attempt to make banjos using wholemeal bread, ciabatta, Marmite, etc., is heresy and will be reported to the Grand Inquisition. A permissible variation for armoured crews is to softboil the eggs in their BVs. This adds tasty razor-sharp eggshell into the mix as a comedy variant.

It's called a banjo because when the yolk and sauce dribble down your front, you move the hand containing the sandwich away and up to a point level with your ear as you look down your front and, usually to an accompanying 'Aw bollocks', wipe/smear the said yolk and sauce into your shirt with your free hand, thus giving a passing imitation of playing 'air banjo'.

[LIVING THE ARMY LIFE] BULLING BOOTS

At best, the average civvy polishes his boots and shoes with two brushes and a tin of polish from the local supermarket, or even one of those 'instant shine' liquid polish applicators. Sadly, this option isn't open in the army. Combat boots are usually greased with a mixture of polish and Nik-Wax, or some similar leather waterproofer, but 'best' boots and shoes, Sam Browne belts and a few other items are 'bulled' to a mirror-like finish in which you can see your face well enough to squeeze your blackheads.

This is one of myriad different ways to bull boots but it's the one I was taught at Sandhurst by my Welsh Guards Colour Sergeant, and it works.

You need:

Two tins of Kiwi ordinary wax shoe polish in the desired colour – usually black. You are going to use one of these for brush polishing and one – which you need to try to keep dust free – for bulling with a cloth and your fingers.
Cold water.
A new yellow cotton duster (flogged in supermarkets in packs of five for about a pound – make sure it isn't impregnated with anything).
A pair of shoebrushes. One labelled 'on', and a soft one labelled 'off'.
And possibly a Camping Gaz stove and a metal spoon.

Theory
What you are trying to do when bulling is to apply a thick layer of polish and then polish that, rather than the leather. It is much easier to get into this Zen-like state of 'polishing the polish' with smooth leather; unfortunately, the army doesn't necessarily work like that and boots and shoes are made from a robust pebbled leather instead. As a general rule, when bulling any leather, DUST IS YOUR ENEMY!

Burning Down
If you've got pebbled leather boots, you're going to need to flatten them. This bit is dirty and stinks, so do it outdoors.
Step 1 Slather the leather in Kiwi polish from your first tin, using your fingers to really make sure it is all covered.
Step 2 Use a Camping Gaz stove to heat up the flat part of your metal spoon handle. You will need to wrap the spoon end in something so it doesn't burn you.
Step 3 Gently press the 'pebbles' flat using the heated spoon handle. DO NOT PRESS TOO HARD! You will burn a hole straight through the leather!
Step 4 Slather more polish on the bits of leather you've just flattened and work it into the leather with your fingers.

The burning down process gets you the flat surface you want, but it also buggers up and weakens the leather, so it's a really good idea not to do it to anything that either cost a lot of money, or you're going to want to give reasonably hard use to later on.

Layering

Once you've achieved your flat surface, you need to start layering up. Start by applying some polish from your second tin with your 'on' brush. Make sure you work it into all the welts and seams. Leave it for a few minutes and then give the surface a quick polish with the off brush. This should remove any dust and provide a basic smooth surface to work on. Now using your tin of bulling polish, pick up some polish on your fingers and spread it over the leather so that you have a thin layer of polish all over the leather. Let this dry out for ten minutes or so, then apply another layer and let that dry out as well.

Polishing

With two layers on, you can begin the bulling process. Remember, what you are trying to do is polish the polish, not the leather, so this requires you to be gentle: do not scrub away like Lady Macbeth trying to wash her hands.

OK, take a clean yellow duster and soak it in cold water, then wrap it round the first three fingers of your polishing hand so that you have an unwrinkled 'pad' of wet yellow duster. Dip this into your bulling polish so that you pick up some polish, and then start gently polishing in small circles on your layered leather.

What's happening now is that you're transferring some of the polish you've just picked up onto the surfaces you have layered, and these tiny amounts of polish are filling in the tiny dents and divots in the polish on your layered surfaces. You are also creating a smooth, waxy surface on your yellow duster and the cold water is reducing friction, thus stopping the polish from melting and thus taking polish off the leather, which you don't want to happen.

Keep working away at this, as gently as you can. Whenever you feel your duster 'dragging', dab it in the polish again and possibly in the water as well. Before too long, a deep shine will begin to appear: don't be impatient! The more layers of polish you put on with the cloth, the deeper the shine will be.

Finishing Off

When you've worked up a thoroughly deep shine, finish off with a new clean DRY duster. Wrap it round the same three fingers and lightly dip it into your bulling polish so that a barely visible amount of polish is transferred. Breathe on your shiny surface and, as gently as you can, run the dry duster over the polished surface to take off the moisture from your breath. This should remove any water drying marks.

Maintenance

Once you have a pair of nicely bulled boots or shoes, it's relatively easy to keep them nice and shiny. To maintain the shine in use, always let the leather dry out if it has become wet, brush off any dust and then layer, polish and finish off as above. Periodically – once a year perhaps, depending on amount of use – it is worth removing all the polish and starting all over again.

ARMY PLACES

BATUS

Gopher: these critters bite your fingers off!

Stands for British Army Training Unit Suffield, a large training area in western Canada used for conducting armoured training up to brigade level. The camp at Suffield is more or less literally in the middle of nowhere; there's a small town outside the camp which houses the married quarters and a few other bits and pieces, but that's it. The weather is interesting: it drops into the minuses a lot in the winter but is stinking hot and mosquito-ridden in the summer. There are other hazards too: moose, coyotes, and even – allegedly, though I've never seen one – bears. Even the small cute animals have a nasty side: a friend of mine got the end of his finger bitten off by a gopher.

If you want to have fun, you have to drive. Medicine Hat is about an hour away, and in days gone by this was the home of the famous 'Sin Bin' and 'Cheetahs' where you were guaranteed a beer, a fuck and a fight. Sadly some moral crusading type became mayor and the town was cleaned up. You can still have fun but it's a bit less Wild West.

Calgary is about a three-hour drive, and this is the place to go if you want the comforts of a big city (as well as big-city prices). Try Joey Tomato's for good scoff served by stunning goddess-like waitresses.

Within the camp at BATUS was a burger bar called the Gag and Puke where you could part with some gold pieces in exchange for a burger that a decent vet could have got back on its feet in two or three days. The delightful staff, when asked for a translation of 'loaded' or 'unloaded' (in a ghastly American accent) replied, 'You want shit on that?'

The best part about a trip to BATUS was the R&R at the end. Squaddies would end up as far afield as Edmonton, Vancouver, Banff, Jasper, Seattle, Los Angeles and, in the case of one desperado, Raoul's Rose Garden in Belize.

BELIZE

'A country the size of Wales with a population the size of Swansea', as a particularly good-looking SO3 G2 used to say while giving the new arrivals' brief on a Wednesday afternoon in the force conference room. Belize is a former British colony situated on the eastern seaboard of the Central American isthmus (that's the bit that joins North and South America). This tropical idyll is the only English-speaking country in the region and is bordered by Mexico in the north and Guatemala in the south and west. Formerly known as British Honduras, it changed its name in 1973. As there is another country in Central America called Honduras, it

was deemed prudent to adopt another name rather than simply drop the 'British' prefix, and Belize was chosen after the river that runs through the main city – the imaginatively titled Belize City. The river is also known as the Sweetwater Canal, though it technically isn't a canal. And for 'water' read 'sewage'.

Belize finally cast off its colonial shackles and freed itself from the filthy imperialist British pigdogs in 1981, and that's when things got a bit scary for its inhabitants. Neighbouring Guatemala began to cast covetous eyes over this Caribbean jewel, and the government went cap-in-hand back to its former masters for assistance. Always quick to lend a helping hand to fledgling nations, especially ones that used to be ours, Her Majesty's Government

BATUS, the big nowhere.

Belize: roughing it at the Hunting Cay OP.

dispatched a flight of Harrier ground attack jets and Puma helicopters to the country, along with a sizeable number of troops. The country was duly garrisoned and protected from the threat of invasion by the Hispanic hordes. Rule Britannia!

And that's the way it stayed until the mid-1990s. It was the sunshine posting to end all sunshine postings, and one that didn't involve too much in the way of danger (unlike today's sunshine post-ings): tarantulas, snakes and the occasional mugger only. It was the closest thing one could get to a recruiting brochure, and most got a slice of paradise, whether they were based at the rather prosaically named Airport Camp or at the outlying camps at Holdfast, Rideau and

This bad boy was in my wardrobe.

Salamanca. Tours tended to last six months and the resident roulement battalion was supplemented by various support arms and the Belize Defence Force. And it was possible to cram an awful lot into six months! Life for the Army was generally good, but not as good as it was for the boys of the RAF. 25 Flight AAC didn't have too rough a time either.

What a posting! Where else could one spend one's weekends diving in the limpid blue waters of the Caribbean? The RAF even laid on a Puma for the weekend haul to San Pedro on Ambergris Cay. You were spoilt for choice. The various outlying cays were a tropical dream come true. Goffs, English, Caulker, all were worth the boat ride, especially in a RPL full of BBQ kit! The delights of Cancun and Chetumal in adjoining Mexico awaited the more adventurous, and the town of San Ignacio near the Guatemalan border offered sundry opportunities for getting laid, pissed, or (usually) both. Ah, the fairer sex! If one was thus inclined, there was no better venue for sampling the questionable delights of a bought-and-paid-for jump than the legendary Raoul's Rose Garden – the only brothel to feature on a BATCO vocab card. $30 for a hump and $40 for the All Night Special, and when one considers the exchange rate (BZ$3 = £1) it was a blimmin' bargain, guv! One would never look at a post-pubescent Guatemalan prostitute quite the same way ever again.

Ah, happy times. An endless rollercoaster ride of barbecues and getting pissed on Belikin in the various unit bars. Off camp there was JB's on the Western Highway. In Belize City there was the Upstairs Café, the Hotel Chateau Caribbean (featured in the movie *The Dogs of War* with Christopher Walken), and the Fort George, a renowned eatery. But the dream was to end. The defence cuts of the mid-1990s dictated that such a desirable posting had to end and British Forces Belize was withdrawn. All was not lost, however. A small cadre remained behind for jungle training, and 25 Flight stayed too, its crews getting some of the most spectacular flying available anywhere. 25 Flight also provides SAR coverage.

The days of the British Empire are long gone, but at Airport Camp the Union flag still proudly flutters among the palms, framed by a beautiful, cloudless, blue tropical sky. Units visiting for brief spells of jungle training can only marvel at what it was like a few short years ago. A far-flung outpost. A relic of our imperial past. Bloody marvellous!

CYPRUS

The island of Aphrodite herself, Cyprus has always been a top posting (apart from in the seventies which saw civil unrest and a move away from the Commonwealth. Oh, and the invasion of the Turks). It offers a challenging work environment, a holiday atmosphere and an excellent forces community spirit.

Despite its position as a top holiday destination, there are still a lot of restrictions on where British soldiers can go. This stems from the brutal rape and manslaughter in September 1994 of Louise Jensen, a Danish tour guide, by three drunk British soldiers, after which many tourist areas were put out of bounds. These restrictions were gradually being relaxed, but the rise in Cyprus's popularity in the 'club' scene (i.e. recreational drug-taking and dancing) has led to some being reimposed.

The main attractions are Limassol and Ayia Napa, but good times can also be had in Paphos and Larnaca. If you're willing to travel there's many a

Keo beer: the taste of Aphrodite's Island.

magic spot dotted around the island with no forces influence at all, enabling you to get away and large it with those holidaying nurses, telling them that you're an Apache gunship pilot on a seventy-two-hour pass.

As for establishments, you have the Western and Eastern Sovereign Base Areas that house both Army and RAF units (there is a resident infantry battalion at each end of the island). The West covers Episkopi and Akrotiri, the East covers Dhekelia and Ayios Nikolaos.

The capital, Nicosia – or Lefkosa if you're a Turk – is the base for UNFICYP operations.

Cypriots have an up-and-down relationship with British forces personnel but the majority will welcome you with open arms. It's a key place to get a duty-free car and they will often let you run around in a Gizzit for a couple of weeks while you find your feet and set up finance before purchasing that fuck-off Pajero you've always wanted.

Things to try:

» Meze – a hundred-course meal which lasts too long and you eat all sorts of shite, but you will love it anyway (apart from the little fish).

» Kokinelli – a real locally produced wine/rust eater. The stuff in the shops is tame compared to the stuff you'll get in out-of-town kebab restaurants. Rumour has it that when tested it contained over thirty known poisons! Anyway, it will get you wankered very fast and will (in 99 per cent of cases) ensure you end up with your head in a bucket.

» St Panteleimon – known as St Pandemonium as it's a hand grenade in a bottle.

» 5 Kings Brandy – cheap as chips but massive-quality brandy. Trust me, your tongue will love you for it!

» Brandy Sours – gorgeous!

» Also try to get on the Keo brewery trip in Limassol – always worth a few pints.

Cyprus – it's for winners!

GERMANY

Deutschland, Deutschland, from the Meuse to the Memel, from the Baltic to the Belt, über alles in der Welt. Famed to generations of British squaddies since 1945 as the land of LOA – a laughable pittance sometimes paid to soldiers and their families when posted outside the UK which leaves the average squaddie with an acute understanding of how Judas felt after being given his bung from Pontius Pilate – cheap beer, nice-looking women (some of whom need to shave more often), tax-free cars, and innumerable brothels, porn shops and sex clubs.

Sadly, the British Army in Germany today is a shadow of its former self, and getting more shadowy all the time. Before the Cold War ground to a halt at the end of the eighties, the 'British Army on the Rhine' consisted of 1st British Corps with three operational divisions (the fourth, which was partly TA, was back in the UK) and all the supporting odds and sods, splattered across northwest Germany like a madwoman's shite. Now we're down to about two-thirds of one division in a very limited number of locations, centred around Paderborn (20 Armoured Brigade), Hohne (7 Armoured Brigade), Gutersloh (102 Logistics Brigade), Herford (HQ 1st Armoured Division) and Rheindahlen (JHQ), with a few other outlying units dotted in between.

Along with the loss of the garrisons, it isn't as easy to train as it used to be. In the decade or so after WW2 the Germans damn well did what we told them to; in the sixties, seventies and eighties there was a real threat from the Soviets to justify us churning the German countryside to mud and accidentally knocking down their barns; but since then it's all got a bit quiet in north-west Europe and German farmers don't want armoured battlegroups rampaging across their asparagus, so we do all that in Poland or Canada.

Still, it's a nifty place to live. Get posted there and you are issued a ration card entitling you to buy unfeasible quantities of whisky, gin, tobacco and coffee every week. Germany itself is an orderly sort of place with well-organized 'distractions' (see above re. brothels, porn, etc.), and you do kind of have the life of colonial settlers, albeit in a country with a continental climate that gets a bit icy in winter.

So Who Are Ze Germans?

They come from a country that only became a nation in 1870/71, about the same time as Italy. Till then they were a bunch of warring principalities. Took the Prussians to pull 'em into line. Once Prince Otto von Bismarck had finished with them they were the biggest, meanest cats on the block in Europe.

Our natural allies, in fact. Very good at fighting, and they make a lot of cars. Germans are on the outside cultured and urbane with cold iron discipline, crap haircuts and weird, weird specs. Watching a German dance, especially a red-headed one, is like watching an Asperger's kid at a school disco get down to 'Come On Eileen' in 1986. They can be found wearing leather trousers, gobbing noodles and sausages, and drinking oil.

Like the British, they retain their original tribal rivalries. Swabians do not view Bavarians as a particularly intelligent life-form – nor Prussians, for that matter. But the utmost contempt is reserved for the way

Austrians speak (it's something like the Dutch attitude to Afrikaans, or the French shaking their heads in bewilderment at their Quebecois cousins).

Unlike the British, Germans are highly organized. Trains run on time. The first snowflake of winter brings forth a grand fleet of snow-ploughs. The bulldozer-created tank roads of WW2 have become the autobahns of the twenty-first century on which you'd better be doing 140mph if you don't want a Porsche or a Beemer ramming you up the arse.

GIBRALTAR

Nuclear weapons storage facility ... only kidding!

Located at the southernmost tip of Spain, or as the locals would say 'located at the southern tip of

the Iberian peninsula', Gibraltar, although a tri-service establishment, is mostly a naval asset. RAF Gibraltar is a shadow of its former Cold War self and mostly serves as a refuelling stop and training area for Air Force assets. The Royal Gibraltar Regiment, which used to be a sort of Home Guard/Militia, is now classified as part of the regular Army, albeit with a local defence role.

The locals are friendly, if a little erratic at times, but on the whole are committed to the British forces as well as the British monarchy. They totally deny any Spanish links or likeness, including the fact that they speak Spanish! Squaddies tend to refer to Gibraltarians as 'Gibbos' (pronounced 'Jibbos'), to which they take great offence, so it's best not used in most circles.

The Rock itself is a wonder to behold and contains over thirty miles of WW2 tunnels. Contrary to popular belief, there are no nuclear warheads stored inside it (or a 'Stargate' for that matter). A popular pastime for personnel stationed there is to run to the summit in one go. This is often followed by either heart failure or a sense of jubilation.

Of particular interest are the amazing wanking monkeys of the Rock. These unbelievably ugly, flea-bitten, aggressive beasts will give the tourist a friendly screech while lazily having one off the wrist. When not engaging in the real thing, the monkeys enjoy a bit of rape/being raped – which involves a whole lot

of screeching by both parties – followed by a bit of post-coital flea-picking, and of course getting the nappa down. It is said that when the amazing wanking monkeys leave, the British will go too. This may well be true, because beyond a bit of simian voyeurism there's not very much to do there.

Gibraltar is a contested territory: Spain wants it (God knows why); Gibraltarians want it to stay British. For the time being it's ours – red telephone boxes, bobbies on the beat, Auntie Betty on the banknotes, in true colonial style. Of course, the word 'colony' is a bit un-PC these days and the former colony and British Dependent Territory was reclassified (again) as a BOT – a British Overseas Territory – in 2002.

THE FALKLAND ISLANDS

Wind. Rain. Sheep. Penguins. Errr … that's it.

The Falkland Islands: brrrrrrr!

COMBAT SERVICE SUPPORT

REMFs (Rear Echelon Motherfuckers)

In the rear with the gear.

These are the branches of the British Army which enable the combat and combat support arms to conduct operations, by delivering maintenance, logistic, medical, administrative, police, training and welfare support. In many respects these are the less glamorous parts of the Army, but even so they are fundamental to its operational success. Sadly, though, they just don't pull the birds – hard luck, REMFs! On the other hand, the

combat services do include a much higher percentage of women who are, according to myth and legend, there for the pulling by bold and brave members of the combat and combat support arms. Woo hoo!

THE ROYAL ELECTRICAL AND MECHANICAL ENGINEERS

Spanners; Spanner Monkeys; Reems

REME is the branch of the Army that fixes things when they get broken. They do this by supplying 'Light Aid Detachments' to units with lots of breakable equipment, and by establishing workshops equipped for various categories of equipment repair at different stages in the logistics chain.

These are formed into seven regular, two 'integrated' (i.e. mixed regular and TA) and two TA battalions.

Regular Army

1. **(Close Support) Battalion REME** – 4 Armoured Brigade
2. **(Close Support) Battalion REME** – 7 Armoured Brigade
3. **(Close Support) Battalion REME** – 20 Armoured Brigade
4. **(Close Support) Battalion REME** – 12 Mechanized Brigade 19 Light Brigade Combat Service Support Battalion – 19 Light Brigade
6. **(Close Support) Battalion REME** – 1 Mechanized Brigade
7. **Air Assault Battalion REME** – 16 Air Assault Brigade

Integrated 'Force Support' Battalions

101 (Force Support) Battalion REME – 102 Logistic Brigade
104 (Force Support) Battalion REME – 101 Logistic Brigade

TA

102 Battalion REME (V) – Regional Forces
103 Battalion REME (V) – Regional Forces

The range of equipment REME is responsible for maintaining is vast, effectively from cooking equipment to Apache helicopter radars, and as a consequence there is a wide range of trades among REME soldiers, primarily including the following:

Vehicle Mechanics, split between A Mech (tracked vehicles) and B Mech (everything else).

Recovery Mechanics, the Army's answer to the AA on the battlefield.

Technical Storemen – Quartermaster staff, and responsible for obtaining tools and special test equipment.

Armourers, who fix guns, anything from pistols to tank cannons. Without them, no one would be able to shoot; with them, no one is able to shoot straight.

Aircraft Technicians, basically glorified mechanics who can fix aircraft.

Avionics Technicians, the god-like figures who can fix all the electronics to keep aircraft flying and fighting.

Artillery Technicians, new in the REME, an Army answer to undermanning: change the name, bodge it, and hopefully fix the problem.

Armoured Technicians – again, new in the REME; same as the Artillery Techs but they work on tanks and warriors to keep them in the fight.

Guided Weapons Technicians, the new name for the old radar techs (hopefully the Army will recruit more due to this name change).

Metalsmiths, who make things out of metal, oddly enough.

Shipwrights, who fix the Army's small collection of sea-going vessels.

Regimental Specialists, responsible for keeping all the tradesmen in touch with their military skills and training (whereas in reality they sit on their Arrses all day complaining about those who actually have a real trade!).

Who Joins?

Looking at the range of trades, it should be pretty clear that dunces need not apply to join REME. Most trades will require GCSE passes at grade C or above, including Maths, English Language and a science. The more technically complex the trade, the more qualifications you will need. Officers are required to have a degree in electrical or mechanical engineering, or a related subject. A point that is well worth taking on board is that it is hard to imagine anyone who has had a successful career in REME ever being unemployed for long after they leave the Army.

THE ROYAL LOGISTICS CORPS

The Really Large Corps; Loggies

The RLC was formed in 1993 to bring the Army's logistics element all together under one cap-badge. The cap-badge itself is of only average size but the corps is vast, comprising about 17 per cent of the Army's total strength. The founding corps were:

The Royal Army Ordnance Corps (aka 'the Rag and Oil Company' or 'the Blanket Stackers'), who were responsible for supplying the Army with materiel.

The Royal Corps of Transport (aka 'Rickshaws, Cabs and Taxis'), who were responsible for moving all the materiel about in their exciting fleets of trucks and even ships.

The Royal Pioneer Corps (aka 'the Chunkies'), who provided a military-trained general labour force, some of whom were even able to spell their own names.

The Army Catering Corps ('Andy Capp's Commandos'), who were responsible for burning food – whoops, sorry! – for providing delicious and sustaining nourishment to keep our girls and boys going.

The Postal and Courier Service Royal Engineers ('Posties'). This was one of those odd anomalies: there was no good reason why this should have been part of the RE other than that they had originally been tasked with setting it up.

The amalgamation allowed the formation of integrated close and general support logistics regiments as well as broadening the scope for careers and postings across the corps. The regular RLC is organized into the following units:

1 **Logistic Support Regiment RLC** – Princess Royal Barracks, Gutersloh

2 **Logistic Support Regiment RLC** – Princess Royal Barracks, Gutersloh

3 **Close Support Regiment RLC** – Dalton Barracks, Abingdon

4 **General Support Regiment RLC** – Dalton Barracks, Abingdon

5 **Training Regiment RLC** – Prince William of Gloucester Barracks, Grantham

6 **Supply Regiment RLC** – Princess Royal Barracks, Gutersloh and Tower Barracks, Dulmen

7 **Transport Regiment RLC** – Catterick Barracks, Bielefeld

8 **Transport Regiment RLC** – Marne Barracks, Catterick

9 **Supply Regiment RLC** – Buckley Barracks, Hullavington near Chippenham

10 **Transport Regiment RLC** – Normandy Barracks, Aldershot

11 **Explosive Ordnance Disposal Regiment RLC** – Vauxhall Barracks, Didcot, with detachments worldwide

13 **Air Assault Support Regiment RLC** – McMunn Barracks, Colchester

17 **Port & Maritime Regiment RLC** – McMullen Barracks, Marchwood

23 **Pioneer Regiment RLC** – St David's Barracks, Bicester

24 **Regiment RLC** – Catterick Barracks, Bielefeld

25 **Training Support Regiment RLC** – Princess Royal Barracks, Deepcut

27 **Transport Regiment RLC** – Buller and Travers Barracks, Aldershot

29 **Regiment RLC** – Duke of Gloucester Barracks, South Cerney

The TA RLC is equally vast and all-encompassing, with units spread across almost all conceivable parts of the UK.

The regular RLC offers the following trades:

Ammunition Technician
Chef
Driver
Driver/Air Despatcher
Driver/Communications Specialist
Driver/Port Operator
Driver/Radio Operator
Driver/Vehicle Support Specialist
Logistic Specialist (Supply)
Marine Engineer
Movement Controller
Petroleum Operator
Photographer
Pioneer
Postal and Courier Operator
Rail Operator
Seaman/Navigator
Systems Analyst

WO2 Kim Hughes GC: huge clanking balls of steel.

It's worth highlighting the first two on this list. You can spot ammunition technicians not by the way they look, but from the sound of their huge balls of steel clanking together as they walk. Their actual role is to inspect, repair, test, store and modify all ammunition and explosives used by the British Army. In addition to these important but relatively mundane tasks they have the lead role in the British Army for rendering safe improvised explosive devices in a high-threat environment – i.e. terrorist bomb disposal. It should be no surprise that the two living GC winners serving in the British Army are members of the Royal Logistics Corps. British ATs (and ATOs – the officers, who do the same job) are the world leaders in high-threat IEDD, and at the current intensity of operations it's likely to remain that way.

As for the chefs, well, whatever you may have heard about SAS selection, P Company and the Commando Course, the reality is that the hardest course in the

[LIVING THE ARMY LIFE] NFI STATES

The British Army has adopted the following ascending scale of NFI ('Not Fucking Interested') states to categorize how deep a soldier is in a Low Interest Entanglement. These reflect a combination of the degree of interest a soldier is likely to exhibit about participating in a particular activity and the degree of interest he ought to be taking in order to preserve his life, career and so on.

- NFI State Low. Typically exhibited by soldiers on patrol in, for example, Al Amarah or Basra, or by RMAS Cadets while being drilled by the Academy Sergeant Major, when a momentary loss of concentration is likely to lead to death, destruction, maiming and so on. No special equipment is required.
- NFI State Medium. Most often seen in soldiers going about their normal daily routine in an operational environment, or taking part in a course. Commanders may need to prepare an L1A1 'Stiff Talking To' in the event that the NFI state threatens to move to . . .
- NFI State High. Usually declared during a soldier's normal daily routine in a non-operational environment, but may also be seen among REMFs on operations. Commanders should consider the alternatives of declaring either (a) a NAAFI break or (b) AGAI 67 action.
- NFI State Black. Is declared during exercises when any NBC play begins or during courses when a Gunner Officer begins a lecture on the role of the Royal Artillery. NFI State Black typically affects all ranks.

Army is the chef's course. We know this because no fucker has ever passed it. Only joking. Army food is pretty good; sadly, the stuff provided in cookhouses and messes by civilian contractors these days often isn't. It seems odd that soldiers should have to deploy on operations in dangerous environments to ensure they get fed properly.

Who Joins?

The size of the RLC means that it can offer something to more or less anyone who joins the Army, whatever their qualifications. The RLC has an undeserved reputation for sweeping up officers who haven't been able to commission elsewhere in the Army, which is probably not true, even though they do have a lot of slots to fill. The reality is that, as in most regiments and corps, you need to be good to succeed.

THE ARMY MEDICAL SERVICES

The AMS consists of four separate corps: the Royal Army Medical Corps, the Royal Army Dental Corps, Queen Alexandra's Royal Army Nursing Corps, and the Royal Army Veterinary Corps. Together, these are able to provide comprehensive primary healthcare services to the Army and its dependents on operations and in peacetime.

It's worth pointing out that the huge majority of officers in the AMS are what the Army calls PQOs, or 'Professionally Qualified Officers'. They do a much abbreviated course at Sandhurst which essentially teaches them how to put their uniforms on, live in the field for short periods, return a salute, fire their personal weapons and a few other basic military skills which might come in handy from time to time. In return for this they are paid at rates comparable with what they could expect to receive in civvy strasse. Nice work if you can get it.

THE ROYAL ARMY MEDICAL CORPS
Pox Doctors; Chancre Mechanics

The RAMC is the largest single cap-badge within the AMS. It provides the Army with the following specialist personnel:

Doctors – GPs, surgeons, anaesthetists, head-shrinkers, the whole nine yards.

Operating Department Practitioners – assistants to surgeons and anaesthetists.

Bio-medical Scientists, who analyse samples of nasty bodily gunk so that you know when you have nerve gas poisoning or chlamydia.

Physiotherapists, who twist and pummel you back into shape.

Pharmacy Technicians, to count out those Oxytetracline pills on a Monday morning.

Pharmacists, to mix the party punch.

Radiographers, to take the X-rays.

Medical Support Officers – either crusty old LE officers recruited from elsewhere in the Army or bewildered young DEs direct out of Sandhurst, who try to manage the whole shebang in the face of medical intransigence.

Environment Health Technicians, or drain sniffers.

Environmental Health Officers, or senior drain sniffers.

Combat Medical Technicians (last but certainly not least), who aren't nurses and aren't quite paramedics (though the Army is working on getting their training recognized towards paramedic status), but certainly a lot more than first-aiders. CMTs are the foot soldiers of the RAMC, often providing front-line care for wounded personnel waiting for and during casualty evacuation.

THE ROYAL ARMY DENTAL CORPS
Fang Farriers; Tooth Fairies

Strangely enough, the RADC fix teeth. In addition to the dentists themselves, who are all officers, the RADC recruit:

Dental Support Specialists (the artists formerly known as Dental Nurses)
Dental Hygienists (professional toothbrushers)
Dental Technicians (false teeth masters)

QUEEN ALEXANDRA'S ROYAL ARMY NURSING CORPS
QAs

Not that long ago, QAs were all women and were the object of the sexual obsession of British soldiers worldwide. It was an essential rite of passage for all British military men to claim to have shagged a QA, and to make the joke that 'There are only two certainties: death and a QA – ha ha ha ha ha!' while everyone else groaned with boredom. QAs were routinely invited en masse to Sergeants' and Officers' Mess parties in the hope that it would all turn into a glorious shag-fest like in Rodox porn videos. Even now it is a widely held belief in the British Army that a ghostly busload of nurses from the British Military Hospital Rinteln roams the North German Plain like the Flying Dutchman, just failing to arrive at parties in time. Now they recruit blokes too and it isn't such a tempting prospect.

There is a limited range of career choices as a QA: professionally qualified nurses can apply to be commissioned; nursing students with confirmed places on nursing degree or diploma courses can apply for sponsorship from the Army at university followed by a commission; Level 1 registered nurses can apply to enter as soldiers; and applicants with the right qualifications can be trained for the Army by Birmingham City University on a registered nurse diploma course. The alternative to being a registered nurse is becoming a 'healthcare assistant', i.e. an emptier of bedpans and a mopper-up of spilled bodily fluids.

THE ROYAL ARMY VETERINARY CORPS

The Army Pets Corps

It's fair to say that the Army's dogs and horses are probably a far more co-operative bunch than the human contingent. One side of the RAVC role is providing veterinary care to those working horses, dogs and regimental mascots, which is carried out by professionally qualified vets and 'veterinary technicians' (i.e. veterinary nurses), but occupying a slightly higher profile at present is the recently formed 1st Military Working Dog Regiment RAVC, which provides search and guard dogs for operational deployments. Dog trainer/handlers are recruited by the Army to develop an unnaturally close relationship with a succession of large'n'loveable canine companions.

TA AMS

Much of the regular Army treats the TA a bit like the embarrassing uncle who turns up at Christmas, gets drunk and tries to grope his teenage nieces – family, but you wish they were somewhere else. Not so with the TA medical services. Recruited from the NHS, TA medical personnel are often at the cutting edge of medicine in their civilian careers and bring immense added value. Oddly enough, the military battlefield medical

[LIVING THE ARMY LIFE] SKIFFING

A tricky one to explain . . . Skiffing is a game played with various degrees of enthusiasm, depending on amounts of alcohol consumed and degree of separation from the influence of home and family – and indeed any of the moral foundations of Western civilization.

Not to put too fine a point on it, the art of skiffing involves the insertion of the skiffer's own index or middle finger in his (or her – skiffing is an equal opportunities pastime) rectum, followed by the use of said befouled digit to draw a moustache, real or imaginary (depending on claggification), on the unsuspecting skiffee. This action is followed by the whispering of the word 'skiff' quietly in their ear. The result may be imagined, thus skiffing is, in practical terms, a test of speed, agility and reaction times. Not bad, eh?

OK, it is. Although, to be fair, it doesn't happen very often. It's included in the *Arrse Guide* just so you know that should anyone rub his or her finger under your nose and whisper 'skiff', do not under any circumstances sniff or breathe in in any way. Ever again. Ever.

system works in pretty much exactly the same way that the equipment recovery and repair system works. Casualties are evacuated through various stages until they reach the appropriate level at which to be treated. Thus in Afghanistan, for example, a minor casualty might be treated by his regimental medical officer and his team, while a more serious casualty would be evacuated back for treatment at Camp Bastion, or back to the UK and Selly Oak. For all the furore about the closure of the military hospitals, the decision to site military medical units in NHS hospitals in the UK has meant that medical and dental personnel are exposed to the most up-to-the-minute techniques, and this has had a real impact on the Army Medical Services.

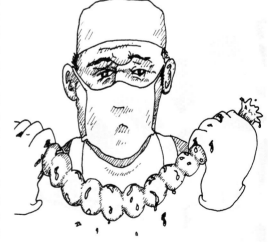

Anyone for tripe?

[LIVING THE ARMY LIFE] BOOZE

As a responsible employer the Army takes a firm line on alcohol: excessive consumption is firmly discouraged and could be a reason for adverse career-fouling reporting.

And yet . . . go into any Junior Ranks Club, Sergeants' Mess or Officers' Mess and you'll find booze on sale not far above cost price; go into the same places in Germany and it's duty-free! Drinking is everywhere in British military culture.

A recent positive trend has been that most overseas operational deployments have been either 'dry' or severely restricted in the amount of booze personnel are allowed to drink. This normally means no wine or spirits at all and a restriction to a maximum of two cans (1 litre) of medium-strength beer per day. In a desert or arid high-altitude environment, that's normally more than enough.

Still, having said all that, it would be foolish to get flouncy about it. One of the staples of the British soldier's life, beer is a simple wholesome product made by fermenting sugars extracted from malted wheat or barley in water and adding hops for flavour. Once matured to improve the taste you have a drink which at its best can set your eyeballs revolving in different directions while you are simultaneously convinced that you are:

- Rambo;
- the Greatest Lover since Casanova;
- the Greatest Singer since Elvis;
- the Greatest Dancer since Fred Astaire (or John Travolta, if you're that way inclined);

- irresistible to all women;
- as witty as Oscar Wilde;
- able to stand.

The broad geographical spread of the British soldier has introduced him to a wide variety of different types of beer from many nations.

In Belize: Beliken beer is brewed just outside the old British Army base at Airport Camp (now mostly occupied by the BDF). Allegedly brewed to taste like Heineken (but in Belize – see what they did with the name there?), it developed something of a cult following. In my opinion it was drinkable without actually being particularly nice. Soldiers posted to Belize also got to sample the various local rums, which could be an interesting experience.

In Canada: Tricky one: it really is a case of quantity over quality in most Canadian bars, unless you find a place which does 'real' beers from Canadian and US micro-breweries, and imports.

In Cyprus: The two great beers of Cyprus are Keo and (locally brewed) Carlsberg, aka Charlie G. Allegedly Keo is drunk by Cypriot socialists, Carlsberg by nationalists. Whatever: both are very acceptable mainstream lagers, particularly when strongly chilled. Keo wines are pretty good too, if you like your reds fruity.

In Germany: In the home of lager, the staple of the squaddie weekend is the Herforder Pils 'Yellow Handbag', an attractive cardboard ten-pack of high-quality bottled beer which can be bought in low-priced multiples from the NAAFI and can easily make a long, lazy weekend seem to flash by in a matter of an hour or two. Strange, huh? Another popular German beer is Warsteiner, aka 'Wobbly'.

One to avoid, in my opinion, is Weltins, to be found around the Sennelager/Paderborn area. It tastes perfectly nice but induces an earth-shattering hangover the next day. Ouch!

In Kenya: Tusker lager has its adherents, but these tend to be people who like drinking something which tastes a bit like sparkling embalming fluid. Kenya-brewed Guinness has an interesting dry flavour, but watch out! It's around 7.5% alcohol by volume and is likely to creep up and give you a severe sand-bagging, in combination with the high altitude.

In Poland: Polish beers tend to have names like Skrzchpflzki or Felch but despite this are generally in pretty much the same league as their German counterparts, with one difference: their eye-wateringly high alcohol content. It's pretty much guaranteed that if you have a post-exercise piss-up after your Uhlan Eagle comes to an end, the ten-hour drive back to BFG is going to be undertaken in a degree of discomfort.

And Back Home . . . There is no specific beer associated with the British Army, but one staple is the various types of Wifebeater.

Seemingly normal lager, Wifebeaters are a type of beer with the specific effect of increasing anger levels as intoxication takes hold. The best known is Stella Artois, but this has been joined by various others, including Carlsberg Special Brew and Kronenbourg 1664, all of which will raise the domestic hackles of the most mild-mannered family man.

According to my last drugs and alcohol lecture, the new one to look out for is Tesco's Strong Lager: cheap as shit, and an eye-watering 8.5% ABV. It is own-brand, so you get that nice blue stripe mark of sophistication, and it takes you out like a pick-axe handle to the base of the skull. It has good 'stormy-ness' qualities as well: four tubes of this and even Gandhi would have been flogging the wife with a length of electrical flex, disciplining the cat with a coal shovel, and piling up and burning all the kids' Christmas presents in the back garden. As a final seal of quality, wherever fragrant gentlemen with unkempt beards are to be found fighting with lamp-posts, you can be sure Tesco's Strong Lager is close at hand.

Bitter: As in the real world, opinion in the Army divides between those who like rich, hoppy southern English-style bitter (bronzed gods sent to live among mere mortals, by and large), and those who like the thin, sour and excessively gaseous northern bitters (whining masturbators with poor skin and questionable personal hygiene almost to a man).

THE ADJUTANT GENERAL'S CORPS

The All Girls Corps; the Army Girls Corps

The AGC was formed in 1992 by amalgamating the Army Legal Corps, the Royal Army Education Corps, the Royal Military Police, the Military Provost Staff Corps, the Royal Army Pay Corps, the Women's Royal Army Corps and the staff clerk branch of the Royal Army Ordnance Corps, thus creating the greatest concentration of REMFs in the history of the British Army. Despite the amalgamation, the AGC is divided into four branches, in order to rationalize what are, in effect, the Human Resources branches of the Army.

AGC STAFF AND PERSONNEL SUPPORT

The Special Pen Service

The AGC (SPS) was formed from the Royal Army Pay Corps and the Women's Royal Army Corps, together with the staff clerks of the Royal Army Ordnance Corps, and the All-Arms Clerks from the remainder of the British Army. Responsible for finance and personnel management, it also provides staff clerks to all sections of the Army, multinational formations and British embassies and high commissions in nearly every country of the world.

Somehow or other, the staff clerk role seems to have diminished in importance. In days of yore, the Chief Clerk G2/G3 in a Brigade HQ could be relied upon to bang out a pretty decent op order if the Brigadier and Chief of Staff were feeling a bit under the weather; nowadays you're lucky if you can find one who knows how to reload a photocopier. Progress huh?

AGC EDUCATIONAL AND TRAINING SERVICES

Schoolies

The AGC ETS is the former Royal Army Education Corps, the branch of the Army credited by some with ensuring that the Labour Party won the 1945 General Election by indoctrinating the field army with socialist propaganda which regular officers and NCOs didn't understand. Nowadays the AGC ETS is populated by officers who can bore the hind leg off a donkey with meaningless management jargon learned on courses at former polytechnics, and failed schoolteachers. For reasons nobody fully understands, AGC ETS officers (there are no 'other ranks') are not regarded as 'professionally qualified officers' and thus do the full Commissioning Course at Sandhurst. While you do bump into them knocking around near the pointy-end of various war zones, the same is true with PQOs. All most odd . . .

Anyway, what they do is provide education, training for promotion courses, personal development guidance and resettlement advice. The basic requirement for officers is a good degree, together with a PGCE or an equivalent education or training qualification.

A typical ETS teacher.

PROVOST

The Provost (pronounced 'Provvo') branch of the AGC now comprises three different parts.

The Royal Military Police
Monkeys; Pigs; Filth; Feds; 5-O

The popularity of the RMP knows no bounds. You can be sure that wherever soldiers gather for fun and entertainment, the RMP will always be there with them, just to guarantee that everybody has a good time. Not.

Actually, most of what the RMP do nowadays is uncontroversial. The days of RMP patrols touring the fleshpots of garrison towns looking for lone squaddies to give a good kicking to followed by a disciplinary stitch-up have long gone. Their formal responsibility is the maintenance of order and military discipline in barracks and on operations, and the RMP will be a visible presence to ensure that this is the case. They detect and prevent crime, control movement and direct traffic, and investigate major incidents involving the Army, ensuring that they do spend a reasonable amount of time getting on everyone's tits, even in these days of consensual policing.

Strangely enough, to get into the RMP you need to get a very high score on the BARB test

If they all looked like this, maybe they'd be more popular.

at the Army Careers Information Office – higher than, for example, the Int Corps and various highly technical trades – although the only other qualification is GCSE Maths and English. As a reward for being unpopular elsewhere in the forces, all RMP soldiers get promoted to Lance Corporal on completion of their trade training.

There are three branches in the RMP. The General Police Duties (GPD) branch are the uniformed, red-hatted basic monkeys, most likely to be seen cruising round garrison towns in blue-light Ford Mondeos, giving squaddies the evil-eye. Alternatively they may be seen on rain-soaked main supply routes being jeered at by the dry occupants of passing vehicles as they monitor and control road moves.

The self-proclaimed elite of the RMP are the Special Investigations Branch (SIB), trained detectives who generally operate in plainclothes in the non-operational environment. Their job is to investigate major crime, conduct long-term inquiries and attend Masonic Lodges. Monkeys become eligible to volunteer for SIB after about five years in the GPD role.

The third branch of the RMP are the close protection specialists. These are the Army's armed bodyguards who look after senior officers, diplomats and politicians in dangerous areas, either in uniform or plainclothes. You can normally recognize them by their garish Oakley sunglasses and the unfeasibly large number of exotic weapons they have strapped to slightly odd parts of their bodies. CP operatives are highly trained and exceptionally motivated individuals whose sole purpose is to make everyone feel uncomfortable and nervous.

The RMP CP course is run at the Defence Police College at Southwick Park, Portsmouth. It is an arduous twenty-eight-day course that consists of rolling out of high-speed vehicles, driving through cardboard boxes, running across rooftops, shooting stuff up, drinking large amounts of whisky and shagging ropey landladies. Course candidates are encouraged to grow their hair and enormous sideys, though moustaches are no longer considered obligatory. CP trainees can often be seen training around the environs of Hampshire, pulling Js and handbrake turns in old Cortinas, Granadas and the odd Jag. CP operatives invariably smell of stale fags and booze and have a dress sense that is questionable – vital attributes that enable them to blend into society in Third World operational theatres such as Leeds. To the initiated, beige slip-ons are the giveaway.

The Military Provost Staff

Formerly the Military Provost Staff Corps, the MPS are the Army's jailers, manning the Military Corrective Training Centre (MCTC) at Colchester. The MPS are all volunteers from other parts of the Army and are selected on the basis of their warm, cheery personalities, soft-heartedness and pragmatic ability to look the other way rather than pick up a prisoner for some trivial offence.

Generations of post court-martial soldiers have used their free phone call to tell their gullible families that they have been lucky enough to be selected for a three- or six-month course at the 'Motor Cycle Training Centre', but surprisingly many of them have returned as better men and women after their period in the warm embrace of the MPS.

Officers of the MPS are all commissioned as LEs from the senior NCOs and Warrant Officers.

The Military Provost Guard Service

Reputedly the Army's response to the RAF Regiment, the MPGS are the fat blokes (and birds) in AGC green berets you see manning the gates at the entrances to major garrisons and bases, with an SA80 strapped across their capacious midriffs. MPGS are employed on a special 'local service' contract which means they don't get posted anywhere unless they want to move.

MCTC: it could be worse.

Qualification to join the MPGS is three years' continuous service in any part of the armed forces, including the TA, RAuxAF or RNR. Their role is opening and closing gates, eating pies and conducting perimeter patrols. Rocket science? Not really, but you get a gun, a badge and a gossip management licence.

HALT! While I finish my pie.

THE ARMY LEGAL SERVICE

The artists formerly known as the Army Legal Corps, these are the Army's lawyers. The ALS are all officers who go through the PQO course at Sandhurst after qualifying as solicitors or barristers. There are about 130 of them, responsible for giving legal advice to the chain of command, supplying training in legal matters for the Army, prosecuting naughty soldiers and giving legal advice to soldiers and their families when garrisoned overseas. A growth area for the ALS since the UK started kicking butt in the Balkans and the Middle East has been supplying advice to operational commanders about rules of engagement and international law, and it's in this role that one is most likely to come across ALS officers in the field army. It's a widely held belief in the Army that any half-decent civilian defence lawyer will run rings round an ALS prosecutor at a court-martial, but don't be too sure!

AND THE REST . . .

Even after the ferocious rounds of amalgamations and rationalizations that have taken place recently there are still a small handful of military organizations that defy easy categorization but which are as much Combat Service Support as anything else.

THE SMALL ARMS SCHOOL CORPS

The SASC recruits suitably qualified Sergeants, primarily from the infantry, and trains them as expert advisers on all things to do with infantry weapons, ranges and range safety. You can't join direct from civvy strasse, and you probably wouldn't want to either.

THE ARMY PHYSICAL TRAINING CORPS

'Once more round my beautiful body . . . go!' PT busters have a similar sort of advisory role to the SASC – although focused on physical fitness, health and sport, obviously – but there are a lot more of them, with most regular major units having at least one on their strength, and Army Training Regiments and establishments like Sandhurst seemingly containing thousands of them, smooching around with oiled muscles bulging beneath their slightly over-tight PT vests. Like the SASC, you can't join from civilian life; instead you need to do the All-Arms PTI course, get some experience as a PTI in parallel with normal soldiering, and then volunteer for APTC selection. Once you're through that, you get promoted to Sergeant and get loaded on to the thirty-week APTCI Class 1 course, ready to begin a career dedicated to making recruits cry.

ROYAL ARMY CHAPLAINS DEPARTMENT

It turns out that I'm not God's gift to the Army after all, but that these guys are. Members of the RAChD are all ordained ministers from Christian churches who have been called by God to minister to his boys and girls in green: which is very nice of him. They wear Army uniforms and officer rank badges but they are not combatants and don't exercise the authority of officers. Chaplains can range from being slightly odd, ineffectual, marginal figures with little influence over the units they serve to strong spiritual leaders who can play a decisive role in the welfare and moral compass of a unit, depending on their personality and their determination to fit in. You don't have to look far to find both types, and every shade in between.

THE CORPS OF ARMY MUSIC

It would be easy to forget that the British Army is probably the biggest single employer of professional musicians in the UK but it is, and this is their parent body. In fact there are 23 regular bands and 21 in the TA, and they employ a couple of thousand very versatile musicians – men and women – most of whom are equally at home playing rock, jazz or swing as they are with military marches. Musicians do a very basic military training to allow them to be deployed into operational theatres, but they are no longer trained as stretcher bearer/medics which was their old war role.

Even if they aren't necessarily the butchest members of the armed forces – I once ran a range for the RA Staff Band and it was like a scene from '*La Cage aux Folles*' – they are great for morale and, if you've never marched onto a parade square with a top military band giving it rock all, you've never lived!

Ooompah, ooompah!

FORMATIONS

As might by now be clear, the British Army is administratively divided into 'units' – regiments and battalions – composed of 'sub-units' – companies and squadrons.

Operationally it deploys in all-arms tactical formations. The smallest of these to deploy for a specific task would be a company or squadron 'group' usually based on an infantry company or an armoured squadron, with attached arms, perhaps a troop of tanks and a troop of engineers with an infantry company, or various other combinations. More realistically, in war fighting and low-intensity operations, units will be grouped tactically in flexible 'battlegroups' commanded by an infantry battalion or armoured regiment Commanding Officer, which might see two armoured infantry 'rifle' companies grouped with an armoured squadron and various other assets, depending on the tactical situation. Easy enough.

Reorganizations and cuts at the end of the Cold War saw the British Army effectively shelving the corps level of command (we now participate in and produce the Commander of the NATO 'Allied Rapid Reaction Corps', but several nations supply the fighting soldiers). Instead, when we go big now we do so only as brigades and divisions.

Brigades A field army brigade is a formation consisting, usually, of two or more battlegroups together with associated 'brigade troops' from the combat support and combat service support arms. Usually commanded by a Brigadier with a thrusting, going-places Major as his Chief of Staff.

Divisions Field army divisions are usually formations of two or more brigades, together with associated divisional troops from the combat support and combat service support arms. Commanded by a Major General, UK

divisions have a full Colonel as Chief of Staff in the headquarters, and unless he really fucks up, his next job will be as a Brigadier.

Regional Forces The British Army also describes its regional commands as 'Brigades' and 'Divisions' but unlike the field army these aren't deployable. Instead, their primary role is the administration and supervision of units based within their geographical area, most particularly the TA, which largely lost its integration into the deployable field army at the end of the Cold War; thus 143 Brigade manages units in the West Midlands, 150 Brigade manages Wales, and so on. The regional Divisional Headquarters are being disbanded as the result of SDSR but the regional brigades will remain to look after their areas. Commanders of regional divisions and brigades are generally highly competent professionals, if not quite as high-flying as the Major Generals and Brigadiers who get given deployable divisions and brigades to play with.

I (UK) ARMOURED DIVISION

1 (UK) Armoured Division is Britain's major surviving war-fighting formation – for the time being at least. It has its headquarters in Herford in north-west Germany but its subordinate formations are based both in Germany and the UK, and the plan is to withdraw all of them to the UK over the next decade. In addition to divisional troops, it comprises:

> **4 Mechanized Brigade** (the 'Black Rats'), based in and around Catterick, North Yorkshire.
> **7 Armoured Brigade** (the 'Desert Rats'), based in and around Hohne, Fallingbostel and Celle in north-west Germany.
> **20 Armoured Brigade** (the 'Iron Fist'), based in and around Paderborn, Sennelager, Gutersloh and Münster in north-west Germany.

THE MOVEMENTS GAME

1 The Movements Game is a game of skill played between the 'Army' – represented by an infantry battalion – and the 'Air Force' team which is selected from part of the RAF movements organization. It is played on a four-dimensional board and involves the transportation of the first team by the second from one corner of the board (the departure airfield) to the other corner (the destination).

2 Play is initiated by an external agency called 'PJHQ'. The unit to be moved and its destination are selected at random, and to achieve maximum surprise and regardless of the actual amount of notice available, teams are to be informed at the last possible moment which allows the move to remain feasible notwithstanding any contrary instructions already issued.

3 When 'Play' is called, each team scores points off the other until the destination is reached, the Army runs out of troops or the Air Force runs out of serviceable aircraft or excuses. The army team can 'resign' from play by adapting its exercise from Brunei to Sennybridge. Points are awarded at the end of each round.

4 During basic planning, the Army scores 50 points if it can persuade the RAF to emplane the unit at an airfield within convenient distance to the unit being moved. The score is doubled if the airfield is devoid of all ground handling equipment and normally confined to light aircraft. The Air Force gains 50 points if the Army is compelled to leave from Lyneham or Brize Norton and bonus points are issued if the road journey to these airfields exceeds the subsequent flight distance.

5 The payload quoted by the Army in planning should in no way resemble the freight actually delivered for loading. The manifests however should be so worded that no formal reproach is possible subsequently between parent headquarters. If the Air Force can identify such a discrepancy it gains 20 points (and 50 points if the correspondence can be escalated to Brigadier level – the lowest level at which a decision can actually be made in the RAF).

6 When allocating aircraft to the airlift, the Air Force gains 20 points for every Hercules it can configure in the full passenger role with a bonus of 10 points if the journey time exceeds 5 hours. The score will be doubled if the Hercules are overtaken in flight by VC10s or Tristars configured in the freight role and carrying the Air Force support personnel.

7 Each team may make full use of conflicting or loosely worded orders, and 20 points will be awarded for any change not acted upon for which the recipients' own administrative service can be found to blame for ignorance of changes to times and place of departure.

8 The time of the Army unit's arrival at the departure airfield and the actual departure of the aircraft will bear no resemblance to any published information. The Army may claim 1 point for every minute by which this time interval can be shortened whilst the RAF can claim a similar score for the unnecessary early arrival of the Army.

9 The Army may be permitted to play a joker by loading freight to the aircraft themselves. The Army will be awarded 50 points for each aircraft loaded on time and about which the Captain and Loadmaster can find no valid reason for insisting on reloading or relashing. The Air Force will allocate troops to individual aircraft and so ensure that no plane contains any recognizable sub-unit of the Army's organization and may claim 1 point for each man separated from his company.

10 Each soldier is to be briefed at platoon, company and battalion level as to his baggage allowance and the list of prohibited articles. Ten points will be awarded to each soldier who exceeds his baggage allowance by more than 20% and a further 10 points awarded for any man who reaches the aircraft steps openly carrying a hexamine cooker, Miniflare launcher or thunderflash.

11 En route the Air Force will be penalized for any unserviceability at Laarbruch or Goose Bay requiring an overnight stop. Points will be recouped if the aircraft can be declared unserviceable at Nairobi, Singapore or Hawaii. The Air Force will gain points if it can persuade the Army to remain in the departure lounge by claiming imminent departure and these points will be doubled if the aircraft can be declared serviceable but then delayed for a further 10 hours because the crew has exceeded its duty time. The RAF can gain a substantial lead if an overnight delay can be arranged. One point is awarded for every soldier compelled to stay in transit accommodation and bonus points are added for each man made to share in excess of the room's normal capacity. The RAF gain further points if they can allocate an officer to the same room as his orderly and score 50 points if, at the same time, the crew secure hotel accommodation in the nearest city with points being multiplied by the number of 'stars' the hotel has been awarded.

12 A prompt arrival is valued exceptionally at 50 points for the RAF. The Army reduce this score for each piece of baggage mislaid and this will usually be a weighting to achieve parity. The RAF can claim 10 points if it can announce that the unit commander's baggage was offloaded en route and 20 points if this proves to be true.

13 On arrival, the scores are compared and if the Air Force wins it begins the return move with a bonus of 200 points. If the Army win they can opt for a return by sea.

3 (UK) MECHANIZED DIVISION

3 Division, with its headquarters in Bulford, Wiltshire, is Britain's second deployable division. It is less armour heavy than 1 Division, but has four manoeuvre brigades in comparison to 1 Div's three:

1 **Mechanized Brigade**, based in and around Tidworth in Wiltshire.

12 **Mechanized Brigade**, based in and around Bulford in Wiltshire.

19 **Light Brigade** ('19 Shite Brigade'), with headquarters in Catterick but units based in Northern Ireland, north-west and south-east England.

52 **Infantry Brigade**, which was a regional brigade brutally converted into a deployable brigade for operations in Afghanistan, much to the horror of the small gaggle of crusty semi-retired staff officers running the place. Fortunately, most of them were posted out and replaced by thrusty young ones – phew! Headquarters in Edinburgh and units based across Scotland and in north-west England.

16 AIR ASSAULT BRIGADE

16 Air Assault was formed from an amalgamation of the old 5 Airborne Brigade – a parachute-based formation – and 24 Airmobile Brigade, which used helicopters for mobility. 16 Air Assault, with its headquarters in Colchester and most of its units in eastern England, now combines highly mobile air assault infantry with the astonishing strike capacity of the Apache attack helicopter. Sexy huh? The manoeuvre elements of the brigade are two battalions of the Parachute Regiment and two battalions of light role infantry in the air assault role combined with three regiments of attack helicopters, all supported by the usual brigade troops, many of whom are parachute qualified.

3 COMMANDO BRIGADE ROYAL MARINES

3 Commando Brigade isn't actually part of the British Army, but it does have quite a few soldiers in it, including 1 Rifles as one of its four manoeuvre elements, 29 Commando Regiment Royal Artillery, and various parts of the Commando Logistics Regiment. Without claiming the power of prophecy, one does wonder whether the Royal Navy will want to cling on to the Royal Marines, including operating a separate recruit and officer training establishment, as the Fleet gets increasingly whittled down over the coming years, or whether they will hand them off in part or as a whole to the Army.

[LIVING THE ARMY LIFE]

REGIMENTAL RESTAURANT

Hahahahahahahahaha . . .
Euphemistic re-branding by the Army of, you guessed it, the cookhouse. In the good old days the Army took a couple of quid off you at source from your pay every day and in return you got to fill your face with as much as you could get away with at breakfast, lunch and dinner. Sure, the slop jockey might give you an earful as you took a second scoop of beans or a third Weetabix, but everyone knew it was swings and roundabouts.

Not a bad system, you might think, and it worked for soldiers, NCOs and officers. And if they wanted a bit extra – like a glass of wine, or an extra course at dinner – in the Sergeants' or Officers' Messes, they paid a bit of 'extra messing' and got it. But Joe Squaddie wasn't happy: he resented having his pay docked for mere food when he

could be out partying, using the extra two quid fifty or so to entice top international supermodels into unrestrained orgies. The Army hierarchy listened to these whinges and, lo!, they acted, introducing 'Pay As You Dine'. To nobody's surprise, this turned out to be shit. The more dimwitted among the soldiery – and there are a few – carried on as before, blowing all their cash in the first couple of weeks of the month, only to find that they could no longer afford any food. The more geeky retreated to their Type-Z accommodation, living on Pot Noodles and other similar shite.

Meanwhile, the traditional Officers' and Sergeants' Mess 'full fry' became a 'core breakfast' featuring one glass of fruit juice, one cup of tea, one bowl of cereal or one egg, one sausage, one piece of toast and one slice of bacon. How shit is that? Very.

THE WEIRD AND WONDERFUL WORLD OF WALTS

If you've read this far, it isn't entirely unreasonable that you might have concluded that some of the benefits of being in the Army are pretty cool but all that bollocks about training courses and dangerous deployments to Afghanistan is a bit of a pain. Never fear, there's an easy way round this! You can mope around, 'holding your manhood cheap' (don't do that in public!) as King Hal might have put it, or you can put your worries behind you and just make it up.

Yes, 'Walting' is an increasingly popular pastime amongst those who frankly can't be arsed to go through the difficult bits. It gets its name from James Thurber's 1941 short story 'The Secret Life of Walter Mitty', about a young man living out a fantasy life. It's a joke in the Army that every pub has at least one ageing, alky regular who claims to have been in the SAS – and most likely one of the leading pair into the Iranian Embassy in 1980 – but more and more fakers and frauds are turning up in British Legion clubs and even on Remembrance Day parades. And they're getting away with it too! The frauds have found that no matter how outrageous their claims – they've 'secretly' won the VC; they've been knighted by the Queen – people are reluctant to call them on their lies because they don't know enough about the military to gauge whether they're for real. Even so, some of the more outrageous examples have been caught out in recent years as the media have cottoned on to this phenomenon.

James Shortt: SAS Walt.

James Shortt built an international business as a security and counter-terrorism consultant on the basis of his supposed background in the Parachute Regiment and SAS before he was exposed on Arrse, the *Sun*, *Private Eye* and elsewhere for having actually been an adult instructor in an Army Cadet Force detachment which wore the Parachute Regiment cap-badge, and having failed the TA SAS recruit training course after a couple of weekends.

Captain Sir Alan McIlwraith's cover was blown by an extensive biography on Wikipedia, detailing his covert exploits bringing peace to the Balkans and the Middle East before it emerged that he was actually a Scottish call-centre worker.

A Beginner's Guide to Successful Walting

But if you really want to know how to get away with it, this is the one-stop shop of everything you'll need to know about how to 'Walt with confidence'. Don't wind up on the front page of the *Sun*, being sniggered at in NAAFIs across the land, but use the experience of others and in no time at all you'll be boring people shitless with tales of slotting jundies in the Stan and busting caps on the ranges at Ponty with Vince, Lofty, Goose and Harry the Hook. Enjoy!

Getting Started

Becoming a Walt is not all glitz, glamour and buying medals off eBay; it takes imagination, quick wits, and hard graft. As a budding Walt, one of the first things you'll have to do is to choose your regiment or corps. This is not a matter to be taken lightly if your

'Sir' Alan McIlwraith: call-centre worker.

aspirations are higher than to become a mere 'pub Walt'. To be a truly convincing Walt it's often best to avoid the more 'high profile' units: SAS, Para and Royal Marine Walting is best left to the gauche and ignorant or the real pros. Remember, there's only ever a couple of hundred SAS soldiers at any one time, and they all know each other. They won't know you.

But if you Walt as an ex-RLC chef, all you need to be able to do is talk about reconstituting mashed potatoes and occasionally shouting 'You there, only two sausages/Shredded Wheat/Weetabix' or 'More pepper!' This will convince all but the most persistent sceptic that you are the genuine article. If any additional proof is required, showing them a Polaroid snap of yourself in grubby chef's whites dipping your cock in a large stock-pot will remove any doubt from their minds.

An Officer and a Gentleman

Another potentially disastrous pitfall is choosing to adopt the old faux officer ploy. Contrary to popular belief, it takes more than a nasal guffaw and questionable dress sense to carry oneself off as a holder of the Queen's Commission. Anyone who has passed through the hallowed portals of Sandhurst, Dartmouth – and possibly even Cranwell too – will be equipped with knowledge of such arcane things as mess etiquette. If you add a shot of bitter lemon to your port or put brown sauce on your Pommes Dauphinoise, you're going to get caught.

Your attire will also reflect directly. It's no use regaling your audience with amusing anecdotes of the time you debagged Ginger in the mess if you look like a pikey in grey loafers. Therefore a decent 'half-change' rig of tweeds, moleskins, tattersall shirt and an appropriate regimental tie is vital. You may wish to complete the image with a Labrador or Spaniel.

However, one thing worth noting is that (like gallantry awards and honours), commissions and promotions are published in the *London Gazette*. That means you're not going to be in it – no matter how burnished your brogues or how pressed your red corduroy trousers are.

You could, however, if you were really desperate to impress, find a common name and trace his or her career path and simply adopt it by changing your name by deed poll. Realistically, all that means nothing if you then start shovelling foie gras down your grid with the wrong fucking spoon! Stick to Other Ranks, it's far easier.

Get Connected

Unless you can rattle off a compendium of bezzers, you will appear to have no muckers. Every unit in the British Army has some (if not all) of the following:

» 'Dinger' Bell

» 'Dusty' Miller

» 'Chalky' White

- » 'Tug' Wilson
- » 'Nobby' Clarke
- » 'Smudge' Smith
- » 'Bunny' Warren
- » 'Teresa' Green
- » 'Strangely' Brown
- » 'Windy' Gale
- » 'Dutch' Holland
- » 'Spike' Jones
- » 'Ned' Kelly
- » 'Swampy' Marsh
- » 'Spud' Murphy
- » 'Nosey' Parker
- » 'Johnny' Walker
- » 'Spider' Webb
- » 'Harry' Black
- » 'Derek' Rigg
- » 'Frankie' Vaughan

Namedropping these will enhance your chances and – who knows? – some may well actually exist and the person you're boring to death may well actually know them. Having memorized them, you're then at liberty to drop them in to the conversation like fine ingredients into a rich soup. 'Nobby? Yeah, top bloke. I remember when Tug Wilson skiffed him in the Mally at Oberammergurgle. Fookin' hilarious it was.' Etc, etc, etc.

Le Waltage

For many budding Walts, pretending to have been in the French Foreign Legion seems to offer the perfect exotic mix of escapism, romance and acting like you're dead hard. It's also difficult to check: Legionnaires may enlist under an assumed name if they choose and so Barry Scrunge of Wigan can easily become Caporal-Chef Hugh Jorgen, International Homme Mysterieuse, if he wants to. If you can speak French, smoke Gitanes Maïs by the packetful and drink red wine in pints, it may be worth a go.

THE WALTING LIFE

Grooming

The experienced Walt will have every minor detail covered. The hair will be just right: not cropped, but not too long either. Sideys are optional but highly recommended. Moustaches are also optional, and whilst the Jason King look is slightly obsolete, a good upper lip-full of hairage is no bad thing. Remember, there's no point in talking yourself up whilst looking like a complete twat.

Home and Office

It goes without saying that one's abode should ideally have some subtle decor that hints at a suitable background. Framed certificates extolling your prowess as a successful, top-of-the-class, underwater, knife-fighting, high-altitude canoeist are best avoided. A regimental plaque – suitably signed on the reverse by 'Bones, Tak, Ginge and the rest of the lads' – accompanied by a photo of yourself and your bezzer (suitably clad) should be enough to do the trick. Remember, you don't have to spend six months in the 'Stan to achieve convincing photographic evidence. A trip to the sand dunes of the Norfolk coast with a set of dusty dessies and DPM on a sunny day has exactly the same effect.

The Wheels

Without a doubt, your choice of mechanical conveyance will pay dividends, provided you make the right one. Wheel-spinning into the pub car park, before J-turning into the parking slot with one swift, deft flick of the steering wheel will do your credibility no good if you're in a Vauxhall Nova. Doing the same in an '85 Range Rover, however, will. Be warned, though: anything green and obviously ex-military will merely make you look like a military vehicle collector: a group of people just one small step above train-spotters in the sad-git league tables.

Talking the Talk

By now, it's assumed one would be conversant with the technicalities of all things Special Forces. You should have read the collected works of both Chris Ryan and Andy McNab, as well as being a subscriber to *Combat & Survival* magazine. If not then get a grip! This is Day One stuff sucker! If you've done your homework correctly, you will be aware that the life of an operator is more than just slotting darkies in faraway lands and bedding fit birds. You need skills. One of these is languages, and the ability to speak in a foreign tongue adds a whole new dimension to your alternative life.

Nothing turns heads like an operator switching effortlessly between his native tongue and some Johnny Foreign jibber-jabber, but be careful. Until comparatively recently, any alien tongue stood out like a tin of Wifebeater in a mosque, but now that the entire country is awash with ~~freeloading bastards~~ welcome guests from every corner of the Earth, the impact is somewhat diminished. This is where your individual skill compensates.

The chances of someone speaking (for example) Azeri in your local pub are greater than they were twenty years ago, but as you're not actually speaking that particular language there should be no problem – unless you say you do, only to find that the person you've told actually does.

Choose Your Target

The real skill in Walting is picking your target: Who are you trying to impress and why? Blurting out your bogus war stories to everyone in earshot down the pub can make you the temporary centre of attention but it is fraught with danger. It's all

[LIVING THE ARMY LIFE] GROWLER

A true culinary delight and staple diet of drunk squaddies, nocturnal barracks prowler sentries and fat Ron Hill Trackster-wearing wives. Essentially a portable heart attack, a growler is a warm, soggy, greasy pie or pasty from a NAAFI vending machine or fast food counter. It will contain suspicious lumps of meat, gristle and fat of assorted colours and textures; its temperature will vary wildly, from nearly frozen through to boiling (soft bits and sauce); and all wrapped in deliciously oily and compressed pastry.

It must be properly served in a paper bag or on a cardboard tray to ensure that the greasiness is obvious to the consumer, who would otherwise think he had been sold a sub-standard growler. Ideally consumed with brown sauce and mustard out of sachets. I once found a human fingernail in one; I suspect it improved the taste.

There are also two veggie options: starve, and fuck off and starve.

about targeting. Once you've acquired the wardrobe and the 1000-yard stare, the obvious target for your blather is the slightly ditzy, easily impressed, blonde nympho-maniac; not the big taciturn guy in the North Face jacket with the walrus moustache. While both may actually give you a sympathy nosh, there's a real danger that Mr Facial Hair is the SSM of B Squadron at Credenhill.

EXTREME WALTING – LIFE ON THE EDGE

For some, simply spinning a yarn is simply not enough and they decide to commit Walticide by throwing themselves to the lions. Should you feel the urge, then great care is required as this is hazardous.

The perennial favourite – the Vietnam POW – is fraught with danger. The US Department of Defense has a complete and exhaustive list of everyone who spent any time in North Vietnamese or Viet Cong captivity, and if you aren't on it – but claim to be a 'Nam POW' – then you're looking at international ridicule on various high-profile websites.

Slightly more frighteningly: falsely claiming to have won the Medal of Honor – or even just owning one (or a replica!) if you haven't been awarded it – is a Federal offence. The FBI will have your back doors in and you'll be carted off to the Federal pen for twenty years' worth of anal re-boring in the ablutions. Blimey!
… it's as simple as that!

[LIVING THE ARMY LIFE] CRIME AND PUNISHMENT

Discipline in the army nowadays is mostly self-discipline. Officers and soldiers are supposed to be well motivated professionals and they shouldn't need to have people constantly on their case to ensure that everything gets done. Yeah, right. The truth is, like all big institutions, a proportion of the people who manage to join are either natural-born fuck-ups who help in the general descent towards entropy and anarchy without any particular malice; or they are the minority of rebels and renegades who fight back against any system, no matter how benign.

The Good Old Bad Old Days ...
I joined up in the days when Centurion was a rank, not a tank, and back then we had, in effect, two systems of disciplinary enforcement: formal and informal. The formal system was straightforward: if you did something relatively minor, a superior might award you some extra-duties or a small fine in kind. If you did something slightly more serious you were charged with an offence under the Army Act and you would then appear on 'orders'.

Orders were a form of summary court-martial. You would be marched in front of your company or battalion commander (for more serious offences): the charge would be read out; you would be asked if you understood it and whether you were prepared to accept the adjudicating officer's decision; you would be asked to plead guilty or not guilty; and any evidence that

was being used would be read out. After this, the officer would then pronounce on guilt and award a sentence. This might be one of a series of warnings about conduct; extra duties; a fine; or even a sentence of detention, during which the individual would also have been deprived of pay. Detention was an uncomfortable experience: it usually meant spending the sentence in a cell in the regimental guard room, being beasted by the Regimental Police staff and doing various forms of fatigue duties around camp.

Of course, the whole process was a stitch-up. 'March the guilty bastard in!', everyone joked before the summary process began. Evidence, guilt and sentence were usually worked out at the same time between the company commander and his CSM, or the CO, Adjutant and RSM, and the only way to circumvent it was to decline to accept the decision of the court and opt for a full court-martial instead. This was a nuclear option – evidence of extreme bolshiness – but in reality sometimes the only way to avoid an unfair punishment. Individuals charged with serious offences, ie those likely to get a sentence greater than 28 days' detention, got remanded for court-martial anyway.

Courts-martial were slightly fairer than summary proceedings, in that legal representation was the norm rather than the exception, but they were still generally convened on the basis that if the accused wasn't guilty, he wouldn't be there.

The informal system was uncomplicated.

NCOs and the occasional officer would suggest to a malefactor that the formal disciplinary system was a needlessly complicated and cumbersome system to deal with a problem which could be easily solved by more direct means, without the risk of fines, detention and/or career damage. If the bad boy in question agreed to this approach, he would be taken round the back of the drill sheds, tank hangar, workshop or some similarly large edifice, and twatted until it was mutually agreed that a lesson had been learned.

The Modern Approach

In recent years, various courts have examined the formal system of military justice and decided that it is wanting in many respects. The consequence of this has been the increasing involvement of the Military Police and their use of Police and Criminal Evidence Act rules in investigating offences which would, in the past, have been dealt with within units.

The net effect was that units became wary of using summary punishments and there was a perception that discipline might suffer because the powers of officers and NCOs to punish bad behaviour were very unclear.

AGAI 67

The Army bounced back with AGAI 67, effectively a set of rules explaining in detail the powers of NCOs and officers to punish minor offences without the need to use the formal disciplinary system. AGAI 67 allows sanctions like show parades, extra duties, extra training and a range of other options – which don't include the inflicting of pain or public humiliation – which are properly recorded, transparent, proportionate and fair.

MCTC Colchester

Of course, the real badasses will still find themselves doing porridge at the 'Military Corrective Training Centre' at Colchester. Journalists call this the 'Glasshouse' but generations of soldiers have told their parents that they've been sent on a course at the 'Motor Cycle Training Centre' and won't be home for the weekend for the next three months. It's an odd place, effectively divided into two wings: D (Discharge) Wing in which those who are getting the boot from the armed forces (it holds naval and air force prisoners too) are given some resettlement training for the civilian world; A Wing, where those who will be resuming their careers are 'retrained' to be good little boys and girls.

If you've seen the film *The Hill*, it isn't like that. Let's be honest, it isn't a touchy feely fun palace, but most detainees find it isn't really much worse than being back in basic training and many of those who knuckle down and try to get on with life find they kinda, sorta enjoy it. The retraining does work too: it isn't unusual for those who've been through MCTC to actually enjoy a career renaissance and earn promotion not long afterwards. Of course, there are better ways to this.

THE OTHER SERVICES

THE ROYAL AIR FORCE

The Crabs; Crab Air

A strange organization with generally unjustified delusions of militarism. Historically very good at getting money out of the government for expensive shiny equipment.

As a service, the RAF closely matches banks, since they are never available after 1630 hours or at weekends. In fact, within the RAF, working on a Wednesday is generally considered a no-no because it buggers up both weekends.

Despite all that they seem to be quite good at the flying thing – well, better than a lot of Johnny Foreigner's air forces anyway. Their most impressive recent feat was to persuade HMG to stump up the cash for about 10,000 Eurofighter Typhoons – an aircraft allegedly designed to replace the ageing Spitfire as the ultimate weapon against Hitler's mighty Luftwaffe – thus completely bankrupting the MoD to the extent that the rest of us will only be allowed to shout 'Bang!' once a year in case we get sore throats.

Eurofighter Typhoon. For each one the government bought, they had to close a children's hospital. Probably.

RAF OFFICERS

Q. How do you know when a pilot enters the room?
A. Don't worry about it, he'll tell you.

Time was when the Officers' Messes of the Royal Air Force were populated by frightfully well-brought-up young chaps who had been to public schools and joined up to engage in chivalrous single combat with the Hun. Back in those days RAF messes were cluttered with attentive working-class stewards ready to bring a large whisky and soda to any young Knight of the Air who happened to have bagged a brace of

Tally ho, old boy!

Sit, 'Dog of Colour'!

Boches, and by black Labradors with names that would give Diane Abbott MP a fit of the vapours.

No longer. RAF mess stewards these days are men who have been fired as British Airways cabin crew for being too camp, while in the RAF lexicon 'dog' is something you do in secluded public car parks alongside Stan Collymore.

Once the chance of dying painfully but heroically in a hail of Nazi 20mm cannon fire was snatched away from them, RAF officers were forced to look elsewhere for that whiff of excitement and adventure . . . and at last they found it by installing one-armed bandits and video games in their Officers' Messes.

Now, after a tough afternoon unloading crate after crate of illegal duty-free booze from the back of his C-130, pausing only to 'tip' the RAF Police with their share, the modern-day Biggles can unwind from the pressures of work by ordering a long, refreshing glass of Malibu 'n' Baileys from the bar and feeding surplus Lithuanian coins into machines in the hope of winning a few quid before heading back to his room to drink lager out of cans and play with his X-Box.

RAF 'OTHER RANKS'

In the Army and Royal Marines it is generally the commissioned officers who send the chaps to do most of the dirty work. In the Royal Navy the officers and the chaps have to do it together on a large floating Exocet target. The RAF is unique in that the chaps stay safe and dry in a nice cosy bomb-proof hangar while the commissioned officers are shot down and given a ferocious beasting on Al Jazeera TV. This is perhaps the reason why some RAF personnel develop a somewhat 'civilian' demeanour.

Even so, just because RAF other ranks don't get to fly very much doesn't mean they can't make their mark in other ways. In fact there are three branches of the RAF which have managed to develop a demonic reputation for pissing the rest of the armed forces off.

RAF Movers

It's the job of movers to get men and equipment from A to B (where A is the start point and B is the destination) as efficiently as possible.

Fly-by-night civilian charter airlines, which briefly come into existence every year with the sole purpose of moving thousands of chavs from Gatwick or Manchester to Ibiza and Corfu, generally find that despite deliberately handicapping themselves by recruiting only recent immigrants with learning disabilities, they can get four hundred or so drunken, unruly civilians checked in and loaded on to a plane, together with all their chattels, in about two hours.

Not so RAF movers: to check in and move a hundred highly disciplined soldiers, whose kit has already been centrally organized, requires that the soldiers arrive at a disused airfield in Gloucestershire some twelve hours before the flight time so that a small ginger RAF Mover Corporal can insult the officers, Warrant Officers and SNCOs, arrange for the RAF Police to confiscate various items of essential field equipment, and pretend to be amazed when reminded that these soldiers need feeding.

After he's 'managed to persuade' the cookhouse to prepare a meal of chips, chips, chips and beans, and ascertained that the passenger list that was faxed the day before is still correct, he instructs the Chalk Commander (usually a junior subaltern who's been jiffed by the Adjutant) that nobody is to leave the building and then disappears for nine hours, probably in order to wank over confiscated *FHM*s while picking his toenails with newly acquired Leatherman tools.

He returns two hours before the scheduled departure time and again checks that the passenger list has not changed, before informing the Chalk Commander that the transport is there to take the troops to the airhead. Transport in this case inevitably means some fucked-up old coaches with seats that are slightly too narrow for fully dressed soldiers who are all

An RAF officers' mess. Probably.

carrying daysacks; also, if the chalk consists of ninety-two pax, there will only be eighty-six seats.

A short journey through the delightful English countryside follows before arrival at Brize Norton where another rude ginger RAF Corporal appears, pauses briefly to insult officers, WOs and SNCOs, and then makes everyone check in again and undergo another hand baggage check, during which even more innocuous or essential items are confiscated as 'Dangerous Air Cargo'.

All military passengers then go through into the 'Airside' waiting area where the Corporal springs

his next surprise: an estimated nine-hour delay. Unfortunately, as you have now been checked in and gone through security you can't leave the terminal. You're stuck there with nothing to eat or drink but Ginsters sausage rolls out of the machine and repellent instant coffee. You aren't even allowed out for a smoke. Occasional glimpses are caught of RAF aircrew in growbags carrying cases of duty-free beer.

Finally the aircraft is ready to board, sleeping soldiers are woken and detritus thrown in bins – at which point the RAF passengers appear. They've been miraculously exempted from having to go to South Cerney and are allowed to report direct to Brize, and they somehow got warned off about the delay so they've spent a few pleasant hours drinking beer in the bar at Gateway House and they're now sufficiently mellow to face their twelve-hour flight to Kandahar with equanimity.

RAF Police

The RAF Police are, among other things, responsible for the security of trooping flights to and from such cultural hotspots as Afghanistan and the Gulf. In this role they take a perverse pleasure in confiscating Leatherman tools and Swiss Army knives from heavily armed soldiers, and X-raying rifles, pistols and other tools of the military trade to ensure that there is nothing dangerous hidden inside them. Another top trick popular with the RAF Police is the confiscation of material that they deem culturally offensive, like copies of *FHM* and *Loaded*, while ignoring magazines like *Vogue* and *Cosmopolitan* which actually normally include more nudity and explicit sexual material.

It will come as no surprise that the RAF Police are not an entirely popular organization anywhere within the armed forces, and that its personnel live in segregation like the nonces in a maximum-security prison.

RAF Regiment

The Royal Air Force even has its own private pretend infantry unit called the RAF Regiment, formed on 1 February 1942. Usually known as the 'Rock Apes', their original role was concerned with airfield defence but this has now expanded into almost any area which they believe might help to justify their existence. The list currently includes:

Manning TACPs (Tactical Air Control Parties) attached to 16 Air Assault Brigade; **Combat Search and Rescue** (CSAR); forming part of the **Joint CBRN** Regiment (Chemical, Biological, Radiological, Nuclear) with two squadrons from **1 Royal Tank Regiment**; training other members of the RAF in military skills (snigger); ceremonial duties; maintaining a parachute-capable **Field Squadron** (II Squadron RAF Regiment); forming part of the **Tri-Service Special Forces Support Group** (a small number of personnel only).

In order to fulfil these demanding roles they have every piece of Gucci kit known to man which has led soldiers based in Iraq and Afghanistan to give them a new title: the Short Range Desert Group.

To be fair, the RAF Regiment aren't bad soldiers at all. Their guys are usually well motivated and well led, but they do tend to make a bit of a meal of it all. Standing outside the terminal building at Basra Airport when one of their patrols has returned, you could be forgiven for thinking they'd just got back from six weeks in the desert harassing Rommel's mighty Afrika Korps rather than a three-hour bimble round suspected JAM mortar baseplates. On the other hand, their devotion to all things Gucci has kept companies like Silvermans and Troopers in business for years, so perhaps we should be grateful for that.

IN CONCLUSION . . .

Even though the RAF aren't very military, we love them really. When the chips are down, they do their bit, even if they do occasionally drop planeloads of 500kg 'smart' bombs on us.

Va-va-voom!

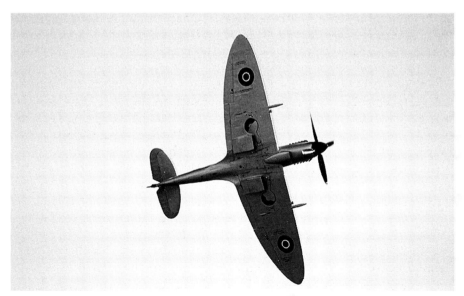

Is that a
roll-mat in
your pocket
or are you
just pleased
to see me?

THE ROYAL MARINES

Booties; Bootnecks

This is the Royal Navy's little military train set, founded way back in 1664 (Kronenbourg have brewed a special lager to celebrate this, probably). For the next three hundred years they provided detachments of soldiers to serve aboard Royal Navy ships in order to shoot albatrosses, carry out keel-haulings, scrape the barnacles off the captain's bottom, and so on. After WW2, as the Empire – and with it the RN – was being drastically reduced in size, they were a bit stuck for a role until they decided to take over the whole 'Commando' gig from the Army which had pioneered it. Thus the majority of Marines are now formed into what are effectively light role infantry battalions specializing in amphibious, mountain and arctic warfare.

To be fair to them, it goes a bit beyond that. The Commando course is a real beast and to get through it recruits and officers need to be highly motivated, fit and determined. In this respect the Marines are not unlike the Army's Parachute Regiment – a self-selecting elite. Officers and soldiers are all trained at the Commando Training Centre, Lympstone.

Officers differ from Sandhurst graduates in that they don't bother teaching them not to scratch their arse-cracks with their fish-knives or peel bananas with their feet, thus many young laydees find it a bit of a trial when first introducing them to Mummy and Daddy. It isn't unknown for the more socially inept Marines officers to try to impress their future in-laws by showing them tricks like the 'white-eared elephant' and 'the last turkey in the shop'.

In addition to the three 'Commandos' – 40 Commando RM (Taunton), 42 Commando RM (Plymouth) and 45 Commando RM (Arbroath), which can operate independently, subordinated to Army formations or as part of 3 Commando Brigade Royal Marines – the Marines do still do 'ship detachments' as well as forming a 'Raiding Squadron' and the core of the Special Boat Service, which is part of UKSF. The Royal Marines' highly regarded ferocity in battle is matched only by their reputation for profound sexual deviancy when on the piss. Cross-dressing is a pretty much routine after-hours recreation, as are naked roll-mat fighting and getting bollocky buff after the equivalent of two sherries (their general nails-ness doesn't seem to extend to the ability to drink). However, even in a frock, high heels and sussies, a Royal is butcher than a Septic Marine in full combat harness driving an M1A2 Abrams tank. If you want volunteers to hang outside an Apache helicopter, fly into a firefight, pull a bud out of trouble and return, then look no further – these are your men!

[LIVING THE ARMY LIFE] MYSTERY FISH

In a dark and deep far-off sea there is a breed of fish that is processed to make the filling for Army sandwiches. No one has ever seen a specimen of this fish in a live state; few have seen it dead and whole. Most of us encounter it only after it has been mashed to a pulp and smeared between two slices of Lidl's Loaf to make a sandwich.

The mystery fish can be grouped in the same category of fauna as the doner, the medium-sized mystery ungulate that is killed and macerated to provide kebab meat. Some speculate that it is not a fish at all but the processed remains of the dead, a bit like Soylent Green. Others suggest that cat poo might be used as a more nutritious (and fishy) substitute. Certainly eight out of ten owners prefer it.

For those of you who deny ever having sampled the delights of mystery fish, or who have repressed the memories, take yourselves to a Sticky Carpet, drink copious amounts of alcohol, trap off with a munter, and when you wake up next to it in the morning, stick your head under the quilt and inhale. Remember now?

Before they get too big-headed, 3 Commando Brigade also consists of a number of Army units and personnel:

1 Rifles
   Commando Logistic Regiment RM (consisting of both RM and Army personnel)
29 Commando Regiment Royal Artillery
59 Independent Commando Squadron Royal Engineers

THE ROYAL NAVY
The Andrew; the Matelots

Hearts of Oak and Jolly Jack Tars to a man – and, in these enlightened times, a woman – the Royal Navy have been the bulwark of Britain's defence for centuries. Hoist the jibber, splice the mains'l and roll out the barrel!

Times change, however. Some now suggest that the glory days of the Andrew ground to a halt a few years back, a state of affairs signalled by the day when they transitioned effortlessly to having more Admirals than ships. In an attempt to buy their way back to military respectability the Royal Navy managed to wheedle the last government into buying them two huge state-of-the-art aircraft carriers to replace the three comedy ones they had built in the 1970s and 1980s, one of which has been stripped almost completely for spares to fix the other two (that's the rather derelict-looking ship you can see in Portsmouth harbour from the deck of Portsmouth-to-Cherbourg car ferries). Sadly, the MoD forgot that somebody was eventually going to have to pay for them. It didn't come as a complete surprise to anybody when the Strategic Defence and Security Review of 2010 decided that while the government couldn't actually back out of the construction contracts, they had no intention of bringing both into use. The first of the carriers to be finished will go straight into mothballs and then be flogged after a decent interval has elapsed; the second will be used but apparently only on a timeshare basis with the French. *Merde alors*!

Even worse for our nautical chums, the quid pro quo for keeping even one of the new super carriers turned out to be losing the crappy little carriers we already had, and with it our entire maritime air capability, at least until HMS *Prince of Wales* is finished. Is that bad? Well, not if we don't have to fight a war against a serious opponent in the next few years. Which is all very well, but history indicates that our ability to predict when we are going to have to go to war is slightly less robust than Mystic Meg's ability to announce the winning numbers for the lottery.

Still, there's always tradition – that great naval (and military) fallback. The Royal Navy can trace its origins back to King Alfred, turning a typically Nelsonian eye to the realities of history. In reality the Crown has maintained a permanent fleet since the reign of Henry VII, but a more realistic date would be the establishment of the Navy Board by his son, Henry VIII, in 1546. The Navy declared for Parliament in the Civil War, but this is conveniently forgotten because when the monarchy was restored it inherited from the Commonwealth a fleet that had been built up to three times its pre-Civil War size.

For the next 350 years they took on all comers and generally kicked their arses, establishing a dominance that was both psychological and actual. In fact the Royal Navy was so badass that in 1940, when we were allied with France and at war with Nazi Germany, they cruised down to

Avast there, me hearties!

[LIVING THE ARMY LIFE]   NAKED BAR

This is the stuff of legend. A popular and enjoyable pastime in the Officers' Mess, particularly when female officers can be persuaded to take part. Alas, this ancient ritual is now under threat, as the result of the leaking of a video of a somewhat barbaric Royal Marines naked barbecue to the *News of the World*.

There are essentially two versions:

- The Fantasy. This typically would involve a scenario in which a limited number of male officers or soldiers find themselves in a bar full of nubile lovelies, perhaps from the women's company at RMAS (what's it called? Sappho Company? I can never remember) or a busload of nurses from Rinteln. After the words 'Naked Bar' are called, the only sound to be heard is the swish of silky lingerie coming off and the snapping of suspenders being released, perhaps enhanced by the odd girlish giggle.

- The Reality. A 'Naked Bar' is called in premises – normally a makeshift Portacabin with nylon carpet tiles – containing forty-seven male soldiers in various stages of obesity, and two elderly visitors from the WRVS. As soon as the first shoe comes off, both women leave. Pints of warm lager are then served to a lot of fat naked men in a room smelling strongly of feet.

Mers el Kebir and Oran and sank most of the French fleet just for the hell of it. This was followed by a series of encounters in which the sausage-noshing squareheads came second, drowning in the North Atlantic shouting 'Teufel!' and 'Donnerwetter!' as the icy waters closed over their heads. Take that, Bismarck! The somewhat quieter post-war era allowed the Royal Navy to develop its expertise in different areas, specifically the cultivation and propagation of exotic venereal diseases. Us soldiers never quite cottoned on to the fact that being in the Navy wasn't all a re-enactment of *The Cruel Sea*. Yes, sometimes they would spend a bit of time splashing around the North Atlantic being sick and failing to find Soviet submarines, but more often than not they were carrying out the important role of showing the flag in gritty war-zones like Singapore, Rio de Janeiro and New York. Showing the flag in these cases generally meant finding the nearest economy brothel and settling in until the money ran out and it was time to go. A Navy medic once told me that supervising the first sick parade after a run ashore was almost enough to put you off sex for ever. Almost.

The Royal Navy's most recent 'finest hour' was, of course, the Falklands War of 1982 when a wide variety of ships were plucked from the shelves of the UK government's secondhand warship shop and sent south to do battle with Johnny Argie. Billed as a confrontation between a Latin American fascist dictatorship and a Western European democracy, in reality it seems to have been a publicity stunt dreamt up by European missile manufacturers. Aerospatiale's Exocet was notably successful at converting Her Majesty's warships into colanders, but BAE Systems' Sea Wolf got an honourable mention for splattering Argie pilots across wide areas of the South Atlantic.

The period since the Falklands has been relatively lean for the Navy. Chasing Caribbean cocaine smugglers doesn't have the same cachet as torpedoing the *Belgrano*, and, although undeniably fun at first, hosing Somali pirates with 7.62mm Minigun fire becomes dull and repetitive after a while. SO, what next for the Andrew? It looks increasingly like they'll have to sit the next few years out, until they get an aircraft carrier again. Still, it isn't all bad: at least they'll have a chance to work out new ways of promoting each other to Admiral.

ROYAL NAVY OFFICERS

Officer training for the Royal Navy takes place at the Britannia Royal Naval College, Dartmouth. Built in the style of an over-elaborate Victorian municipal public lavatory, it introduces the Snotties to all the strangenesses of naval life. It's very noticeable that the Royal Navy insists on continuing with its own clunky private vocabulary, where kitchens become 'galleys', stairs become 'companionways' and bedrooms become 'cabins'. At Dartmouth, the potential RN officer is taught to use this counter-intuitive jargon at every opportunity, thus having a conversation with a naval officer is a bit like watching someone repeatedly throwing a bowling ball on to a ping-pong table.

It's a sad fact that the Royal Navy is pretty much automated these days and much of the modern naval officer's business would be better handled by a thirteen-year-old with an X-Box 360, but some traditional skills are still taught. Astral navigation, knot-tying and basic boatmanship are still grist to the modern Hornblower's mill, as is learning how to masturbate safely in a hammock.

Unlike the Royal Air Force, where the officers develop about as close a relationship with their airmen as the average motorist develops with the staff at his local branch of Kwik-Fit, Royal Navy officers do have formal leadership responsibilities through the division system which gives them something to do in between taking turns to crew the last few remaining boats.

THE JOLLY JACK TARS

Apart from commenting on their profound sexual perversity, there is little to be said about the sailors of the Royal Navy. It is strongly rumoured that even the heterosexual ones were a bit flummoxed and put out when women were first allowed to sail aboard HM ships. Having said that, as a group Wrens are reputedly the best-looking female service personnel – it's probably the uniform – and there doesn't seem to be the same taboo against them bonking officers to further their careers as there is in the Army. In fact, I once met one whose previous job before joining up had been dancing in a bikini in a cage in a Liverpool nightclub, and her mate said she fancied me . . . ooh er!

HEROES OF THE ROYAL NAVY

Drake, Raleigh, Nelson, Hood, Blake, Rodney . . . the list of great British sailors who have laid waste the Dons, the Frogs, the Boches and latterly the Argies goes on and on, and seemingly was destined to do so into the future. Until that fateful day in March 2007 when a boarding party of sailors and Royal Marines from HMS *Cornwall* was confronted by an

[LIVING THE ARMY LIFE] FISH AND CHIP[S]

'Fish and Chip' is how members of the Household Division – the Foot Guards and the Household Cavalry – describe all other parts of the Army (i.e. the bits they don't consider posh); how members of line cavalry regiments describe all other parts of the Army apart from the Household Division; how members of all line infantry regiments describe all other line infantry regiments and all other parts of the Army, apart from the Household Division and the line cavalry; and how members of Royal Horse Artillery regiments (apart from 7 RHA, who would really have to be taking the piss) describe members of field artillery regiments.

You might think from this that the Army can be socially snobbish, and you might be right, but it's actually a whole lot better than it used to be and snobs now represent a tiny and largely derided minority.

Alternatively, Fish and Chips is the comedy version of the FIBUA acronym (Fighting In Built Up Areas): Fighting In Someone's House and Creating Havoc In Public Spaces.

Iranian speedboat in international waters in the Persian Gulf and before you could say 'Sink the Bismarck!' meekly surrendered and was taken into Iranian custody. Royal Naval jaws and buttocks clenched in shame a few days later when it emerged that Able Seaman Arthur Batchelor, that mighty Corsair of the Seven Seas, blubbed 'like a baby' when some scrofulous Iranians took away his iPod and told him he looked like Mr Bean. Oh the humiliation.

So, despite the fact that the Royal Navy are the sole guardians of Britain's strategic nuclear deterrent, facilitated Britain's victory in the Falklands, and have been generally kicking arse for the best part of five hundred years for King/Queen and Country, we in the Army regard them as a bunch of soft dwarfs who wet their pants at the sight of an Iranian speedboat. Which seems entirely fair to me.

One of these Naval heroes didn't cry when his iPod was taken away: can you guess which one?

APPENDIX:
MULTI-LETTER ACRONYMS

TLAs (Three-letter Acronyms) replaced obsolete TLAs (Two-letter Acronyms) after WW2 when it was realized that the forces needed more possibilities than TLAs allowed.

Both TLAs have now largely been surpassed by MLAs (Multi-letter Acronyms). TLAs are technically abbreviations, whereas MLAs provide an open-ended opportunity for total new-word overload. This appendix features a selection of MLAs for use on a wide range of occasions, all of which will be understood by a military audience, although some are slightly more formal than others.

A
AFV – Armoured Fighting Vehicle
AGHW – All Gone Horribly Wrong
ARAB – Arrogant Regular Army Bastard (cf. STAB)

B
BAG – British Army (Germany)
BALO – Brigade Air Liaison Officer
BAOR – British Army Of the Rhine
BATSU – British Army Training Support Unit
BATSUB – British Army Training Support Unit (Belize)
BATT – British Army Training Team
BATUK – British Army Training Unit (Kenya)

BATUS – British Army Training Unit (Suffield)
BCR – Battle Casualty Replacement
BER – Beyond Economical Repair
BFG – British Forces (Germany)
BFOT – Big Fuck-Off Tent
BJAFO – Basically Just A Fucking Observer (2nd Pilot)
BKYC – British Kiel Yacht Club
BLR – Beyond Local Repair
BOHICA – Bend Over, Here It Comes Again!
BOO – Battalion Orderly Officer
BOS – Battalion Orderly Sergeant
BSFAO – Best Suit For All Occasions

C

CEFO – Combat Equipment Fighting Order (obsolete, superseded by PLCE)
CEI – Communications Electronic Instruction
CEMO – Combat Equipment Marching Order (obsolete, superseded by PLCE)
CES – Complete Equipment Schedule
COIN – Counter Insurgency
CPV – Civilized Patrol Vehicle (NI, early nineties)
CQMS – Company Quartermaster Sergeant
CRA – Commander Royal Artillery
CRE – Commander Royal Engineers
CTF – Chuffed To Fuck
CTR – Close Target Recce

D

DADAFA – Deputy Assistant Director of Absolutely Fuck All
DALO – Division Air Liaison Officer
DARE – Defence Acronym Research Establishment
DCTA – Defence Clothing and Textiles Agency
DE – Direct Entry (Officer)
DFT – Don't Fucking Touch
DILLIGAF – Do I Look Like I Give A Fuck
DMSU – Divisional Mobile Support Unit
DSDA – Defence Storage and Distribution Agency
DSDC – Defence Storage and Distribution Centre
DSO – Did Something Outstanding

E

E4a – Specialist RUC Squad
EOD – Explosive Ordnance Disposal
ERV – Emergency Rendezvous (also Electronic Repair Vehicle)

F

FAC – Forward Air Controller
FEB – Fucking English Bastard/Bitch (for the Jocks out there)
FEHA – Force Environmental Health Adviser
FIBUA – Fighting In Built Up Areas
FIPAC – Fighting In Pubs And Clubs
FIWAF – Fighting In Woods And Forests
FOO – Forward Observation Officer
FOS – Foreman Of Signals
FPF – Final Protective Fire
FRU – Force Research Unit
FRV – Final Rendezvous/Fast Reaction Vehicle
FUB – Fucking Ugly Bastard (as in 'that man's a FUB')
FUBAR – Fucked Up Beyond All Recognition
FUP – Forming Up Point

G

GIFA – Great Iraqi Fuck All
GOC – General Officer Commanding
GPMG – General Purpose Machine Gun
GPS – Global Positioning System
GTF – Get To Fuck
GTT – Gunnery Training Team

H

HALO – High Altitude Low Opening
HLS – Helicopter Landing Site
HMSU – Headquarters Mobile Support Unit

I

IED – Improvised Explosive Device
IEDD – Improvised Explosive
    Device Disposal
IO – Intelligence Officer

J

JAFFA – Just Another Fat Fucking Administrator
JANFU – Joint Army Navy Fuck Up
JEWT – Jungle Exercise Without Trees
JSAT – Joint Service Adventure Training
JSPC – Joint Services Parachute Centre

K

KISS – Keep It Simple Stupid
KTC – Kiel Training Centre

L

LE – Late Entry (Officer)
LMF – Lacking Moral Fibre
LOA – Local Overseas Allowance
LPC – Leather Personnel Carrier (boot)
LRDG – Long Range Desert Group (WW2)
LSW – Light Support Weapon

M

MARINE – Muscles Are Required, Intelligence Not Essential
MBE – My Bloody Efforts
MFP – Mixed Fruit Pudding
MID – Mentioned In Despatches
MPI – Mean Point of Impact
MRF – Military Reconnaissance Force
MUPPET – Most Useless Person Pirbright Ever Trained

N

NAAFI – No Ambition And Fuck-all Interest
NBC – Nuclear, Biological, Chemical
NEWD – Night Exercise Without Darkness
NEWT – Not to be Employed With Troops
NFI – Not Feckin' Interested/Not Feckin' Invited
NFQ – Not Feckin' Qualified (describes a recruit)
NORWICH – (K)Nickers Off Ready When I Come Home

O

OBE – Other Buggers' Efforts
ODTF – Operation Doomed To Failure

OGDW – Operation Gone Disastrously Wrong
OMO – Old Man Overseas

P

PDTF – Project Doomed To Failure
PENIS – Planning Exercise Not Involving Soldiers
PLCE – Personal Load Carrying Equipment
PLONC – Person of Little Or No Consequence
POA – Point Of Aim
POETS – Piss Off Early, Tomorrow's Saturday
POL – Petrol, Oil, Lubricants
PONFU(W) – Personnel Of No Fucking Use (Whatsoever)
PONTI – Person Of No Tactical Importance
POW – Prisoner Of War
PPPPPPP – Prior Preparation and Planning Prevents Piss Poor Performance (aka The 7 Ps)
PTI – Physical Training Instructor
PUFO – Pack Up, Fuck Off

Q

QMSI – Quartermaster Sergeant Instructor
QRF – Quick Reaction Force

R

REMF – Rear Echelon Motherfucker
RLC – Really Large Corps
RSP – Render Safe Procedure
RTU – Returned To Unit
RUC – Royal Ulster Constabulary

S

SCRDE – Stores and Clothing Research & Development Establishment
SH – Support Helicopters
SHPRAC – Squashed Head Practice (Round)
SLR – Self Loading Rifle, 7.62mm UK-built FN FAL (obsolete, replaced by SA80/IW/L85)
SMG – Sub-Machine Gun
SMIG – Sergeant Major Instructor Gunnery (RA)
SMIS – Sergeant Major Instuctor Signals (RA)

SNAFU – Situation Normal, All Fucked Up
SOE – Special Operations Executive (WW2)
SOUP – Single Officer Unnecessary Purchase
SPTA – Salisbury Plain Training Area
STAB – Stupid/Stinking TA Bastard
SUIT – Sight Unit Infantry Trilux (obsolete, replaced by SUSAT)
SUSAT – Sight Unit Small Arms Trilux
SWAT – Some Weekends and Tuesdays (TA)

T

TA – Toy Army
TCH – That Cunt Hoon (as used by the Chief of the General Staff and his mates, no less!), referring to the former Secretary of State for Defence Geoff Hoon
TEWT – Tactical Exercise Without Troops
TFIB – Token Female In Battalion (obsolete)
TOT – Time On Target
TPU – Timer and Power Unit
TULIP – Totally Useless Little Irish Person
TWOK – Tested Working OK

U

U3 – Utterly Utterly Useless
UDR – Ulster Defence Regiment
UMIN – Ugliest Man In NATO
USMC – Uncle Sam's Misguided Children

V

VCP – Vehicle Check Point
VOL – Vision Of Loveliness

W

WCS – Worst Case Scenario
WFM – Whole Fleet Management
WMD – Weapons of Mass Destruction
WOFTEX – Waste Of Fucking Time Exercise
WT – Wireless Telegraphy

Y

YofS – Yeoman of Signals

ABOUT THE AUTHOR

Des Astor realized he wanted to join the British Army while watching the Bloody Sunday riots on television in 1972. Commissioned into the 2nd Battalion the Loamshire Regiment in 1975, he has since served in troublespots across the globe, ranging from Basra to Blackpool. As OC HQ Company of the Loamshires, Des oversaw the merger with the Royal Blankshire Regiment and went on to serve as second in command of the newly formed 4th Battalion, the Amalgamees (Blankshire and Loamshire) (V) before their conversion to a TA RLC catering regiment in 1996. After a successful tour as SO2 G4 (Pest Control) in HQ MND (SE) at Basra International Airport, Des is now at the MoD, as executive officer for a project seeking to implement operational rat-catching protocols across all three services.

Educated at Badger's Heath College near Oswestry and the Royal Military Academy Sandhurst (where he passed out 247th out of 251 in the Order of Merit), Des now lives on the border between Hampshire and Wiltshire with his wife Fenella and their seven Springer spaniels. They have two grown-up children. In what little spare time he has, Des enjoys bricklaying and canasta.

The Author in contemplative mood

ACKNOWLEDGEMENTS

If it hadn't been for Arrse, I would, in all likelihood, have spent the better part of the past eight years surfing the internet for military-themed pornography – although, on reflection, that might have been a more productive use of my time. Nevertheless, deep gratitude is due to the COs, Good and Bad, who have allowed me to take the site's name in vain and produce this book. Equally, I would like to thank all of the very many Arrsers whose wit and wisdom has contributed to this volume, however inadvertently.

At Transworld, I would particularly like to thank my genial editor, Simon Taylor, together with Phil Lord, Katrina Whone and designer Nick Avery, who have combined to forge my semi-delirious mumblings into this roller-coaster ride of laughter, tears and skiffing. Andrew Lownie agented with impeccably suave panache.

Finally, on a more personal note, my dear lady wife Fenella has been my constant companion these past twenty-four years (apart from the time she went off with her tennis coach), and has sustained me through the writing process with gentle encouragement, savage abuse, Eccles cakes and British sherry. Thanks, darling!

PICTURE CREDITS

All illustrations and photographs supplied by the author unless otherwise acknowledged. Every effort has been made to obtain the necessary permissions with reference to copyright material. We apologize for any omissions in this respect and will be pleased to make the appropriate acknowledgements in any future edition.

Page 9: FilmMagic/Getty; Page 14: Arrse; page 15: WireImage/Getty; page 16: Lady Butler: page 17: Arrse; page 19: Lawrence Skuse; page 26: Lawrence Skuse; page 39: BAE Systems plc; page 40: Gary Stedman; page 42: Gabriel Villena; page 50: Daniel Crawshaw; page 62: Arrse; page 68: Arrse; page 69: Arrse; page 71: Arrse; page 77: Arrse; page 78: ISAF; page 82: Arrse; page 83: LAW80/Lawrence Skuse, Milan/Arrse; page 84: top/Arrse, btm/Lawrence Skuse; page 85: top/Daniel Crawshaw, btm/FN Herstal; page 86: Robert Sutton; page 89: SIG; page 132: BBC; page 134: Gary Stedman; page 135: Lawrence Skuse; page 136: Daniel Crawshaw; page 137: Lawrence Skuse; page 142: Lawrence Skuse; page 143: Joey Parton; pages 144/5: BAE Systems plc; pages 148/9: BAE Systems plc; page 156: Arrse; page 163: Arrse; page 166: Daniel Crawshaw; page 167: top/Daniel Crawshaw, btm/Robert Sutton; page 181: btm/BBC; page 183: top/BBC; page 185: Arrse; page 193: Arrse; page 201: top/BAE Systems plc; page 203: Arrse; page 206: ISAF; page 212: Arrse.

Thanks to Archer and Viv de Haan for the temporary loan of the dog and the horse.